GNOMES AND GARDENS

GNOMES
AND GARDENS

by
Alan Melville
Illustrated by David English

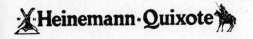

Heinemann/Quixote Press
10 Upper Grosvenor Street
London W1X 9PA
London   Melbourne   Toronto
Johannesburg   Auckland

SBN: 434 98041 2

Printed in Great Britain by
Redwood Burn Limited, Trowbridge, Wiltshire

to
MIDGE
the lady of the house.

Contents

Preparing the Ground

Our England is a garden, and such gardens are not made
By singing "oh, how beautiful!" and sitting in the shade.

I KEEP GETTING this sepia-tinted picture of Kipling (not
the cake man, the poet) knocking off these lines in the
summer-house with a stiff chota-peg in easy reach,
while Mrs K.—the former Caroline Starr Balestier,
American beauty and ex-socialite—is on her knees
weeding the herbaceous border and worrying about
her arthritis. And trying to work out how come God
(with Whom her old man seems to be on the best of
terms) allowed dandelions to have roots as long as the
road to Mandalay, if not longer. Roots, what is more,
which just when you think you've got to the bottom
of them give that infuriating little snapping noise
which means you haven't, and that in a few weeks the
Teraxacum officinale will be back, tougher and more
bloody-minded than ever. (*Teraxacum officinale* is the
Latin botanical name for the dandelion; it has, of
course, been called a lot of other things over the
years.)

My sympathies, naturally, are with Caroline. It
can't have been much fun, after lugging the
wheelbarrow all the way down to the compost heap at
the far end of the garden, to have been married to a
guy who came out with cracks like

1

. . . and when your back starts aching and your
    hands begin to harden
You will find yourself a partner in the Glory of
    the Garden.

Especially if, having come out with it, he poured
himself another zonker and went back to the summer-
house to write "If". Personally, I'd have crowned him
with something from the rockery before he got the
length of "you'll be a man, my son!"

At the same time, there is a great deal to be said for
Rudyard's position—or any enviable position like it; a
deck-chair under the copper beech, say, with the
notches as near the horizontal as possible, watching
someone else get on with it. I am a keen gardener, but
not over-keen. If Louis XIV had been busy, perhaps
with a mistress or two, I feel I would have been
splendid telling *le Nôtre* just where I wanted the yew
hedges planted or reminding him that it was about
time he mulched the orangery. Or, as one of the
landed gentry a little later, summoning Capability
Brown to the conservatory and asking him sharply if
it was beyond his capability to let me have a lettuce,
preferably not one in need of a heart transplant, to go
with the cold left-over venison.

In the absence of a *le Nôtre* or a Capability Brown,
even of a Mrs Kipling, I am a DIY gardener; and like
most other common-or-garden gardeners I put off the
doing for as long as possible. The lady of the house
may keep hinting—*does* keep hinting, in fact; non-
stop, once she warms to the subject—that it's surely
high time something was done about all that black

spot on poor old Ena Harkness. She's absolutely right; there is no point in arguing; it *is* high time something was done about it. But it is also high time for snooker or darts or Pro-Am golf or Jan Leeming or some other cultural activity on BBC2; and as Ena is already looking like a dalmatian on heat, the feeling is that one more day really won't make all that difference.

You will have gathered that this is not a book for the expert gardener. I doubt if Bill Sowerbutts or Professor Alan Gemmell of Keele University will glean anything from it to make them revise their views on pruning mature laterals or analysing that stuff we used to use so much of before John Innes bagged the market. (Earth, remember?)

It is not even a book for the knowledgeable next-door neighbour who leans over the fence and says you do know, don't you, that all that pale greeny-grey stuff on your peonies is peony wilt, and if you don't start spraying 'em regularly with dichlofluanid he wouldn't give much for their chances next Spring; and while he's at it, what are all those dirty brown patches on what used to be the front lawn before you bought the property from poor old Mr Cartwright who was a proper gardener if ever there was one, God rest his soul? (I have a ready answer for that last one. I keep quiet about the dachshund having to nip out last thing at night to do its jobs; I tell him the dirty brown patches are fairy rings, woven by Titania and the other fairies who have risked a one-night stand at the bottom of my garden, and guaranteed to ward off couch grass, moles, and bloody annoying next-door neighbours. It does no good, of course; he's back leaning over the fence next evening, saying I do know, don't I, that the trouble with my broccoli is either whiptail or boll weevil and what I want to do is give 'em a good douche of sodium molybdate solution or better still by the look of 'em, dig 'em up and buy a nice clean cellophane-wrapped colly in Tesco's.)

If it's for anyone, this is a book for the ordinary, impractical, inexpert gardener; the one who gets a vast amount of pleasure out of a garden—and more if someone else mows the lawn and trims the edges; and who—if he's anything like me—is lazy, a cheat, and when the occasion demands it, an accomplished and downright liar. Lazy in putting off what ought to be done about poor Mrs Harkness's domino effect; a cheat in pointing to the border of annuals in full bloom and saying, "Not bad, eh, all from a packet of seeds?" ... when in fact you've nipped over to the nearest nurseries, bought a box apiece of antirrhinums, ten-week stocks, French marigolds and lobelia and bedded them out under cover of dark on the night you knew the neighbours on both sides were at Bingo.

And downright liars ... well, I once admired a glorious display of delphiniums in the garden of a famous lady novelist who (though no publicity slouch, she) must on this occasion remain nameless. "But, darling," she said, "they're the easiest things in the world to grow. They're easier than *cress*. You just pop them in and forget all about them and—*voila!*..." The very next person I spilt the tepid Veuve de Vouvray over was, of all people, the President of the Delphinium Society and one of the

4

country's leading delphiumnists. "She's such a delightful woman," he said. "I let her have a selection of our prize varieties every year, and of course I send over one of our chaps to see they get the right mixture of rich, well-drained soil and give them a touch-up with thiopanate-methyl once a fortnight in case of mildew."

Shakespeare wrote of "no gentlemen, but gardeners"; the rest of us talk about gentlemen farmers, but never gentlemen gardeners. Why should we? We're all liars. When the grass is so high that for once you can't see the daisies in it and you've just noticed the enormous thistle which is so big that you missed it altogether when weeding the rose-bed, I have heard myself say with burning sincerity, "but I *like* the garden looking like this. I *hate* a regimented garden where the parsnips are exactly five inches apart in a dead straight line, like guardsmen on parade along the Mall. After all, dammit, even on State occasions at least one guardsman goes queasy at the knees and falls flat on his face, usually just when the Obo of M'bobo is passing and Ma'am is obviously wondering what to give him for lunch. It ruins the straight line, but what the hell? It shows they're human, or at least in need of a drink. I like a garden to look *natural*, the way Nature intended it." And should anyone try to counter this line of thought by drawing a comparison between Nature's intentions and something out of *Quatermass*, just remind them that *Quatermass* did very much better in the ratings than, say, *Brideshead Revisited* with all its immaculate lawns and well-kept borders.

The first garden I tended or left unattended was a

section about five feet square at the rear of the house in which I was born up in Northumberland. It was bordered by a trim little box hedge which my mother cut with her nail scissors and was known, not very wittily, as Alan's Little Patch. It contained nothing but Virginia stock and groundsel; the first because it is easy to grow (and sometimes a twopenny packet of the seed was given away Absolutely Free with the gardening periodicals); the second because it is difficult to stop it growing.

The next one was on virginally unresponsive land on a new housing estate, also up in the northernmost tip of Northumbria; it involved bribing a farmer friend to put a plough through the whole thing before one could even take a pick-axe to what appeared to be outsize bits of Hadrian's Wall. Cabbage was then put in over the entire estate in the mistaken belief that it "cleared the ground"; for two years everyone ate cabbage, either plain boiled, as a sort of north-country version of cole slaw, or in bubble-and-squeak if enough potatoes could be found to cope with the plethora of greens.

Just when I got the garden along the Tweed valley looking, I thought, rather nice—and had dug the first new potatoes and started putting on airs about picking my own raspberries before picking anyone else's—I came south to London and was reduced to a window-box. I did a broadcast about it in, I think, "Woman's Hour"; it was in the late thirties, and I still get letters from what must be very old ladies asking how the geraniums are getting on. The window-box was at the top of Shaftesbury Avenue, where it joins with New Oxford Street; James Agate, the drama critic, lived in the flat below and kept complaining about the drips when I watered it. It was the only time, I'm happy to say, that he gave me a bad notice.

Then there was the war; *then*, greatly daring, I bought an allegedly Regency house in an allegedly Regency terrace in Brighton. It had a sizeable garden and for the first time I felt I could do adventurous things, like growing orchids in the greenhouse. This was a disaster; the orchids were splendid and I was in great demand at weddings, but the temperature at which the greenhouse had to be kept was such that everything else, myself included, wilted. And the bills were astronomical. Now I have what I suppose would be called a town cottage, or to be more truthful (this is the unacceptable face of capitalism) two town cottages, one on each side of the road. One has a walled garden much given to honeysuckle and old-fashioned rambler roses and considerably less than the size of a tennis court, *and* a greenhouse; the other has a front patch not much bigger than Alan's Little One, and at the back of the house what was described by the estate agents as a "sun-drenched south-facing patio."

When I was shown over by the rather ashen young man from the estate agents I said, "But this isn't a patio—it's a back passage." The ashen young man ricochetted back and clutched for support at one of the many drainpipes; he then said—going more ashen than ever—"The properties on our books, sir, do not have such things as back passages." This was in Brighton, mark you; not Hove.

Never mind: with several gallons of pure white paint and some slightly bogus bright red Spanish-style tiles and with fuchsias in hanging baskets and standard roses in tubs and pendulum begonias dangling from the most questionable openings in a slightly chipped stone cherub on near-marble plinth and with window-boxes on all available ledges, even the one which prevents the kitchen window from opening, it gives me a great deal of pleasure. As, in fact, have all the gardens or parts of gardens I have from time to time neglected. It is still, however, referred to as the back passage. It's a form of inverted snobbery or class-consciousness in reverse gear; "Do come and see the nasturtium up my back passage" sounds somehow more forthright and down-to-earth than "Do come and see the magnolia on the patio."

It's not enough, really. I mean in the way of qualifications for writing a book, however impractical, about gardening. I have, however, one genuine claim to horticultural fame. I am a begonia. Or was.

Several years ago, when I was doing much too much television and as a result was more of an *objet*, if not *d'art*, *de notoriété* than I am now, Messrs Blackmore and Langdon of Bath—probably the world's leading begonia cultivators—wrote me saying that each year they introduced three new varieties of begonias, and would I agree to having one of that year's trio named after me? Well, of course, I was thrilled; it put me, after all, on a par with Ena Harkness, black spot or no black spot. Either Mr Blackmore or Mr Langdon (they are to begonias what Mr Steptoe and his associate are to test-tube babies; and obviously charming characters, exuding old-world courtesy) wrote again saying that of the current

9

year's threesome one was a delicate pale lemon with picotee edging, which they didn't feel was really me; the second was a pure white single bloom with faint blush pink centre, which again they didn't feel was me; but the *third* was a hardy, outsize, long-flowering brilliant scarlet which both Mr B and Mr L felt was me to a T. So I appeared in the catalogue, at £3.75 a tuber, no less. (I came down pretty swiftly to £2.50 and was last heard of as a sort of remainder job lot at 50p each, or £4.25 for ten of me, p and p extra, but inclusive of VAT.) They even sent me a dozen of myself with the compliments of the management; I still have them, and it's quite something to be able to admire yourself without being accused of narcissism. Begoniaism, perhaps.

But ... not so long ago a friend of mine (actually a composer with whom I had worked on several shows but with whom, unlike many of his predecessors, I was still on speaking terms) bought a property in the purlieus of NW1 and found himself for the first time in his life the owner of a fair-sized garden. Plus what I have no doubt his estate agents described as an attractive sun-drenched loggia; the very place for the important gardening operation known as Bringing Things On. What better house- or loggia-warming present, I thought, than a dozen of me? So again I wrote to those charming gentlemen in Bath, and got this back:

We are in receipt of your letter of the 17th inst., with enclosed cheque which we are returning herewith.

We find this extremely embarrassing, but it is

with very great regret that we have to inform you that you have proved completely infertile and of no use at all for breeding purposes. You have therefore been removed from our catalogue and are no longer available.

If your friend would be interested in receiving any of our more reliable begonias—or perhaps a selection of our many prize varieties of phlox, gloxinia, or hand-pollinated polyanthus—we shall be happy to carry out your instructions.

It's the story of my life, really. One day you've your name in lights—or on a begonia—the next, you're papering the spare room with rejection slips and worrying about your virility.

About the other half of the title of this book—Gnomes—we are on even more insecure ground. I had better come clean right away: I am not what you would call a dedicated one-hundred-per-cent gnome-devotee. I've really nothing against them; I just feel there is already enough potential trouble in a garden without having one of those smug, self-satisfied, rosy-cheeked little bastards squatting year after year after year at the edge of the goldfish pond pretending he's fishing. Or pushing a tiny little wheelbarrow, still with that idiotically contented smile on his face. Who, in God's name, ever kept on smiling while pushing a wheelbarrow?

The lady of the house, on the other hand, is pro-gnome. She knows that she would be running the risk of being hit over the head with a spade if she dared infiltrate one of them even behind the shaggy *Ligustrum ovalifolium* in the front garden; she gives expression to her odd kink by inserting very small gnomes round the house plants. At regular intervals these are noticed, removed, and put in the dustbin; a day or two later, when you decide to water the sparmannia, you find another little horror has arrived, wearing yet another bright green jerkin and scarlet balaclava and with the same inane happy beam on his face.

Don't be deceived by that beam. I know this sounds stupid; I have no concrete evidence to support the theory and I'm sure it's something I should have flushed out of the system long before now, but in my view there is a slightly sinister side to a gnome not yet recognised even by the most avid gnome-collector. Especially after dark. I have an uneasy feeling that after dark gnomes—some gnomes, at any rate—get up to things which are, to use a favourite expression of my mother's, not quite the clean potato. The fact that they squat on their allotted sites all day, beaming away, harmless as harmless—it's a front, a facade, a cover-up job. No wonder they've that grin on their faces; they're thinking of what they're going to be up to after nightfall. Next time you're passing a gnome just after dusk, take a quick look; I'll bet you'll find its expression has changed. There's one in a garden not far from my house which I swear the other night had started moving just before it saw me, when of course it nipped back into position and put on its innocent beam again. I know that even to suggest such a thing will land me in trouble with the gnome-lovers; and they're an awkward lot when roused.

Only once have I dared take serious anti-gnome action, and I've never known such abuse. It was once again back in those butterflies-in-the-stomach television days; long before your time, but I did a long series for the BBC called *A to Z*. And in each programme—I was very much younger, of course; and like the sober man Tennyson wrote about, my youth was full of foolish noise—I attempted an impersonation, usually of other notorieties also appearing regularly on the box. In one of the *A to Z* shows I did a character called, inevitably, Percy Throwup; he was giving his expert advice on What To Do With Gnomes. I did my best to capture the rustic accent, getting in as many "ar's" as possible; the gist of his advice was that you dug "an 'ole, see, loike so, see, mebbe three spits, mebbe four spits deep, then you took an 'eavy spade, loike this 'ere, see, placed your gnome on an 'ard surface, loike so, see, ar, an' smashed the little perisher into as many pieces as possible, see, ar, loike so, an' then buried the bloody thing deep in your 'ole, see, 'eeled it well in 'ard, loike, an' 'ope you'll never set eyes on 'im again, never in your natural, ar."

The filming was done in the back garden in the allegedly Regency terrace in Brighton; for years after, when digging it over, bits of little green jerkins and scarlet bonnets kept coming to the surface. The present owners of the house are still coming across them; I think they believe they are valuable Roman remains or portions of priceless pottery of the Yang dynasty. I haven't had the heart to tell them the truth. The programme brought in more vituperative letters than even I had ever received before; I had never realised what an enormous and ferociously loyal band gnome-lovers are. Or what a range of invective they could come out with when someone dared profane the worship of gnomery.

So we must be very careful. I must do research on gnomes. I must try to see the better side both of gnomes themselves and of gnome-addicts; I must be more understanding of the—to me—macabre practice of putting a plaster-of-Paris replica of an obviously retarded midget next to a splash of aubrietia in the rockery in the honest belief that it makes the place look friendly and homely and, well, lived in. It is going to take some doing, but I shall try. But if the lady of the house sneaks one up my back passage there will be trouble.

There are absolutely
  Definitely
And quite understandably
No fairies at the bottom of my garden.

I've concealed myself for hours
In some horrid cauliflowers
In the hope that I'd eventually spot 'em
But each fairy and each elf
Says quite firmly to itself
"I shall not go *near* that ghastly garden's
   bottom".
Not a banshee, troll, or dryad,
Not a leprechaun or naiad
(It doesn't really matter how you name them)
Has ever left its card in
The bottom of my garden
And, being frank, you really cannot blame them.

There's a sordid heap of vegetable matter
Which gives off a strong and unattractive smell.
There are empty tins galore,
Broken bottles by the score—
But one never gets a glimpse of Tinkerbell.
No elfin feet will e'er go pitter-patter
Around my garden's bottom, I'm afraid;
And one cannot blame a sprite
For rejecting out of sight
A place where rhubarb leaves are so decayed.

There's a cesspool filled with green and stagnant
   water;
There's a broken fence with yards of rusty wire;

There are fourteen million flies
And one can't express surprise
That it's not a spot the little folk admire.
Although at times I've seen the gardener's
    daughter
Go down there—on occasions with a friend—
I have never noticed Puck
Weaving spells through all the muck
Which amasses at my garden's nether end.

There's an ancient pair of boots, and lots of
    nettles.
It is dismal, dreary, dirty, dank, and drab.
It is not the sort of thing
Where you'd find a fairy ring
Or expect to meet Titania or Mab.
There are several old and battered pots and
    kettles.
It's a scene that's reminiscent of the blitz.
For a fairy, it's unsuited.
As McEnroe, J. would put it—
The bottom of my garden is the pits.

Which is why there are absolutely
Incontrovertibly
And without a shadow of doubt
No fairies at the bottom of my garden.

Pests

MOST RESORTS—CERTAINLY the one I live in and which I am determined shall be my last—have changed over the past decade; the towns may still be beside the seaside, but they are no longer seaside resorts. The same nice little families no longer spend the same fortnight in the same boarding-house or small hotel, trudging down each morning in either too tight or too floppy plimsolls to the same stretch of beach and trudging back in the evening, hot and sticky or drenched to the skin, for the same meal of huss, chips, and Queen of Pudding.

They go now to Majorca or Marbella or even Miami, and their place has been taken by a steady, all-the-year-round succession of conferences and conventions and congresses and, I suppose, con-men—very good for business but, my God, if you're taking the dog walkies along the front when they spill out for elevenses, *dull*. Four thousand TUC's, either trailed by or scampering after the media, followed on the next Monday morning tide by four thousand Conservatives or Rotarians or micro-chippers or oceanographers (or NUMs, NURs, NUTs, NUPEs, COHSEs, ASLEFs, or SOGATs): week after week

after week, all identikits.

From time to time the delegates at one or other of these jamborees voice a complaint—usually, in the case of the TUC, about the scarcity of Newcastle Brown Ale in the taverns—and threaten to hold their next annual binge in Blackpool or Scarborough or some other more enlightened northern spa. But there is one very important, large-scale annual convention which up to now has shown no sign at all of moving on to pastures new. This is the yearly get-together of NAATAGP (National Association of Aphids, Thrips, and Allied Garden Pests).

The delegates swarm in early in the year, the actual date depending on the weather; sometimes they are delayed by late frosts, but arrive even more determined and resolute in their aims by being kept hanging about before getting down to business. Unlike, say, the Labour Party Conference or even an ecumenical assembly of ARCIC (Anglican-Roman Catholic International Commission), there is no sign of a policy split or a divergence of opinion about what they are setting out to achieve; not a murmur of dissent from some leafhopper Judith Hart or mealybug Ian Paisley. They have their plan of campaign worked out to the last floribunda, and certainly their agenda is a great deal briefer and more to the point than that of the TUC:

19

1. This Conference RESOLVES to endorse the policy of the Executive Council in its continued and sustained attack on all flowers, fruit and vegetables in private ownership; and calls on all fully paid-up members to redouble their efforts, acting either individually or collectively, to bring about the dissolution and eventual destruction of all such unwarranted examples of capitalism at a time when millions of aphids and their associates and fellow-travellers are underfed, ill-nourished, and without recourse either to charitable aid or social security.

2. The Conference DEPLORES the excessive profits made in the past financial year by the privately-owned chemical industry through the development and marketing of sprays, powders, pellets, etc., designed specifically to frustrate the efforts by members of this Association to uphold the principles of freedom and democracy, especially on the underside of leaves of newly-planted young standard roses where there is more chance of getting away with it; and CONDEMNS the continued violation of human rights as laid down in the Geneva Convention by acts of unprovoked aggression against our members who after all are only trying to keep body and soul together by having a quiet nibble at the lettuce. (A separate resolution in the name of the Clack's Farm branch of NAATAGP, endorsed by the NSPCSS (National Society for the Prevention of Cruelty to Snails and Slugs) calling attention to repeated annexation of territory by the manufacturers of "Slugger-Off", the new guaranteed snail and slug

deterrent, is included on p. 17 of the appendix to this agenda.)

3. This Conference UNANIMOUSLY APPEALS to the Secretary-General of the United Nations to take immediate action against the continued assault on aphid liberty by gardeners, allotment-holders, the heavily-armed juntas controlling municipally-owned public parks, etc., and calls for an immediate cease-fire of all aerosol sprays, canisters of methalon dust, derris powder, BHC, etc., and all other weapons of chemical warfare.

4. The Conference, bearing in mind the Association's motto "Breeding Will Out", DEMANDS an immediate increase in family allowances to keep in line with inflation; and unanimously applauds the recent statements by Pope John Paul II concerning the sanctity of life from the moment of conception and the evil of taking any action which might discourage or annul the sexual act.

5. The Conference AGREES that at the conclusion of its deliberations all members shall proceed forthwith to the various target areas allocated by local or branch secretaries and get cracking.

No need, really, to put in that bit about "various target areas". What they mean is my garden. They all come here. If ever I left one of those visitors' books with the column headed REMARKS on the staging in the greenhouse, I can imagine the comments of a satisfied, well-fed clientele ... "lovely digs"; "highly recommended for the family outing"; "breakfast in bed every morning—*yum*!"; "superb vegetarian cuisine, well worth a detour". "Cuisine", you will note; never "grub".

Like most unions, NAATAGP has been strongly infiltrated by the Militant Tendency; the most militant of its members include:

Green-fly. You knew, of course, that the green-fly—as well as being a member of NAATAGP— is a member of the hemiptera family and if they're at all normal, and neither transvestites nor glue-sniffers, they possess (to quote the *Encyclopedia Britannica*) a pair of abdominal tubes or cornicles through which a waxy secretion is passed *and* in certain cases (the *Aphis rumicis*, for instance) a sweet "honey-dew" solution which is voided through the anus—enough to put you off honey-dew melons for life and just the sort of thing that sets off Mrs Mary Whitehouse writing another letter to *The Times*.

You will find this uplifting information in the encyclopedia under *Aphides*, pl. of aphis (and who in God's name ever came across a singular aphis?) and sandwiched between *Aphemia* (loss of speech, which is what happens when words fail you on discovering that Elizabeth of Glamis is smothered in hemiptera) and *Aphonia* (manifestation of hysteria, which is what sets in when you also discover that some two millions of the little bastards have each had quintuplets in the short time your back was turned while trying to find where the lady of the house has put the nozzle for the watering-can). The encyclopedia goes on to say that "the life-style and reproduction of aphids is of a remarkable nature"; surely one of the most sweeping understatements since Churchill said he found de Gaulle difficult to get on with.

The sex-life of the average green-fly is not a bit like yours or mine. Thank goodness. According to the last census, and it must have been a difficult census to take, in the early spring one female green-fly gives birth to 87,648 strapping young green-flies, *all female*; a fortnight later (ten days if it's warm weather) all 87,648 of the kids are at it themselves, each one giving birth to another 87,648 aphidettes, all raring to go and take after mum or gran. This goes on all summer, with ICI and Fisons really the only people happy about the sequence of events. If green-fly spoke scouse, their private lives would surely have been made the basis of a television serial long ago.

How do you know you've got 'em? Here is a practical test, never known to fail. Run your forefinger and thumb gently up the stem of a (preferably thornless) rose; if, having done so, you find eight hundred of the little breeders embedded under each of your finger-nails, you've got green-fly. So, of course, has the rose. So, if you just put your specs on and take another look, have all the roses in the bed and in all neighbouring beds. And, with any luck, the beds in the next-door gardens on either side. You are, as Antony said, "bay'd about with many enemies"; when he added ruefully "millions of mischiefs", he clearly had on his mind not just Cleopatra, but hemiptera.

And how, more importantly, to get rid of the damn things? The more serious gardening tomes advise regular spraying with such easily-pronounced concoctions as dimethoate, formothion, and either oxydemeton-methyl or pirimiphos-methyl. Readily obtainable from all good gardening centres or High

Street multiple stores; just nip into Boots on a Saturday morning when the place is packed and say to the assistant: "I think what I'm after is the small size oxydemeton-methyl—or do you suppose the pirimiphos-methyl might be better, because we've reached the stage where the lady of the house has started flicking either real or imaginary green-fly off the back of her left ear and the budgerigar is scratching so much she's gone clean off her millet?" Better still, sell up. Move to a high-rise flat in NW1 with no window-box and not a sign of an indoor plant. And if anyone offers you an African violet for Easter, refuse it.

Red spider mites. These are the ones who keep going slowly up and down in mid-air like lethargic yo-yo's, without any visible means of support but obviously hanging on to *something* higher up. It is no use making horizontal scything motions in the hope of cutting the poor little mite adrift from its moorings; all that happens is that it disappears completely for a few minutes and when you next turn round it's back at it, behaving like the FT Index. You will know you've got red spider mites by a yellow mottling of your upper leaf surfaces, followed by a general discoloration and eventual death; if you haven't any of these symptoms, you're lucky. You've only got froghoppers or perhaps leaf gall.

The good news about the red spider mite is that it can be effectively dealt with by an anti-red spider mite predator known colloquially as phytoseiulus persimilis (ask for that one, too, when you're in Boots) which has about as much respect for the red spider mite as Tony Benn has for most of Fleet Street.

The bad news is that unless you're a member of the Royal Horticultural Society or having an affair with a research chemist who specialises in phytoseiulus persimilis, you can't lay hands on it for love or money. Better leave the things to go on going up and down in the greenhouse, edging nearer and nearer the pagoda-like erection containing "a profusion of luscious all-the-year-round strawberries" (*sic* and !). Anyway, by the time you can do anything about it, you can buy a half-pound punnet of Israeli ones in the shop round the corner for 65p.

Slugworms, wireworms, eelworms, sawflies, leafhoppers, leaf-cutter bees, etc. These are the riff-raff who concentrate on the few parts of a rose-bush which the green-fly can't be bothered with. They leave the leaves looking like Brussels lace or, in determined cases, a sieve; this prevents the rose from getting black spot, there being insufficient room between the holes to get a spot in. The affected parts (i.e., the whole rose-bush) should be generously sprayed with methalon dust. This has an unusual farinacious effect, causing passers-by to pause and think what an odd time for the lady of the house to make next Christmas's mince pies and then shake all the flour off her hands, apron, and baking board out in the front garden. Not to worry; within minutes of generous spraying, a sharp downpour of rain will remove all traces of methalon and leave the leafhoppers, sawflies, etc., to carry on as though nothing had happened.

Caterpillars and ladybirds. Despite the fact that caterpillars are menaces and ladybirds among the gardener's staunchest allies, these two are bracketed together in our establishment as highly suspicious undercover agents operating against the West. A year or two ago—no doubt it happened to you, too—we had a plague of those fat, rather self-satisfied hairy caterpillars. They got into everything: the lilo, my briefs (hanging on the line on washing day, I mean, not while being worn), a trifle left to cool on the kitchen window-sill, and even on *Nationwide* and in the *Sunday Times* colour magazine. The medical profession issued dire warnings about letting the hirsutes loiter when crawling over any part of the anatomy considered at all personal. But in our pad the plague took on a much more serious international dimension.

It was at a time when, outwardly at any rate, we seemed to be on moderately good terms with the USSR, something which always fills the lady of the house with foreboding. Very quiet they've been lately, haven't they, all that Russian lot? You mark my words, they're up to something. (She was nervier than usual, having been reading too many *Reader's Digest*s and seen a re-run of *Jaws*.) When the hairy caterpillars arrived, all was clear. Psychological warfare, that was what it was. You can't tell me, she kept telling me, that all those hairy caterpillars weren't sent over here in specially camouflaged refrigerated containers and let loose on us to undermine morale; you had to hand it to the Kremlin; up to every dirty underhand trick, that lot were; poor little Carter (he was in at the time) hadn't a chance against them; for one thing, he was a Baptist. Those were no ordinary caterpillars out there, don't you give her that; one night she even lowered her voice, looked round to make sure the dachshund wasn't listening, and mouthed the word "nuclear". She stretched it out the way Edith Evans elongated "handbag".

It so happened that the hairy caterpillar plague was followed by a deluge of ladybirds; no use telling the lady of the house that ladybirds did their level best to destroy pretty well every known garden pest except perhaps the next-door neighbours' children. They— the ladybirds—were a carefully planned follow-up campaign, ramming home the psychological effects of the caterpillars; probably smuggled over here in diplomatic bags for the Russian Embassy. The rear walls of our house, which—unless they need touching up *again*—are normally a gleaming white, turned bright scarlet with the rash of ladybirds; there you are, you see, red as red, they're even sent over here from Nijni-Novgorod or wherever flaunting their national colour. The more we swatted or flicked them off collars and nylons, the more convinced was the lady of the house that her near namesakes, like the caterpillars, were part of a Machiavellian scheme thought up by Gromyko to take the mind of the West off what was going to happen in Afghanistan.

Apart from swatting and flicking, ladybirds should be left alone and allowed to get on with it; in the case of caterpillars getting on top of you, first get out from under them and then get a man from your local pest control office. Or try to. When we rang them, we were told that we didn't think, did we, we were the only people with hairy caterpillars and we'd have to go on the waiting-list like NHS patients in need of an X-ray.

To be fair, five weeks later a nice little man showed up armed with a sort of miniature flame-thrower; by which time the caterpillars had gone. And the Russians had more or less seemed to agree to resuming the Salt II talks. The lady of the house said she didn't like the sound of it one little bit.

Snails and slugs. The product "Slugger-Off" has already been mentioned. It is, of course, a fictitious name; but there are any amount of genuine preparations on the market, all guaranteed to send snails and slugs packing at a rate equivalent to Sebastian Coe running with a following wind. The one the snails in my garden like best—let us call it, just in case of a libel action, "Snail-Away"—comes in the form of small crystallised pellets which you sprinkle round the polyanthi, preferably on the sort of moist evening when snails like to get a spot of exercise.

My snails *adore* "Snail-Away"; they're mad about it. The moment the news gets round that another sprinkling of the delicacy has happened, they converge at breakneck speed from all quarters and lap it up. Runners are sent scuttling off to spread the good news to friends and relations in neighbouring gardens... "You'll never believe it, but the silly old poop's put down some more of that scrumptious 'Snail-Away'" ... "You're joking" ... "Absolutely true, dear, cross my heart: saw him with my own eyes scattering the entire contents of the jumbo-size carton all over the top bed" ... "He's a dear, isn't he?—kind, thoughtful, considerate" ... "Well, come on, don't just stand there, I'll bet Speedy Gonzalez in No 24 is halfway up the wall already, and you know what he's like when there's a free meal going." A couple of hours, and there's not a sign of a "Snail-Away" pellet; if they've any appetite left, the poor things have to fall back on the polyanthi for afters.

The only certain way of getting rid of snails is to pick them up individually—or, if they've been getting ideas from the green-fly, conjointly—and, using a strong over-arm action, throw them over the wall into the next-door garden. If you have a very strong over-arm action, throw them into the next-door-but-one garden. This is safer: any resultant ill-feeling will be between the owner of the next-door garden and the owner of the one next-door-but-one, and you can start throwing the snails in the opposite direction over your other wall.

Cats; sparrows and starlings; small boys, etc. It's odd, isn't it, that while endless complaints are made about dogs fouling pavements, hardly a word is said about cats leaving the pavements spotless but making what the Germans call a Hundenfrühstuck (dog's breakfast) of people's gardens. The trouble with cats is that they are tidy, fastidious creatures; the havoc they wreak is not through actually performing on the larkspurs but in their commendable efforts to cover up the evidence, digging up so many other larkspurs in the process.

Pepper dust is supposed to be the thing; but the pussies in our neighbourhood treat it with a lofty disdain. I think they honestly believe the stuff is put down to make the going easier on their pads. Broken glass is effective until they learn to pick their way daintily between the jagged bits en route to their favourite depository; it doesn't take them long to

learn. But the broken glass technique is worth persevering with: order in a case of, say, the Sancerre '79; after consumption, smash up the empty bottles into small pieces, using a heavy spade and standing well back; then insert the pieces, sharp edges up, in the flower-beds. It doesn't do any good and it makes the beds look awful, but at least you've had the pleasure of drinking all that Sancerre. Should the cats persist, as cats are inclined to do, order in another case. Repeat if necessary.

Protecting seedlings from *sparrows and starlings* is, according to tradition, best done by weaving an intricate pattern of black cotton thread over the threatened plants. *Black* thread, remember: the argument being that the birds won't see it. If you've ever watched a gull suddenly swoop down from a quarter-of-a-mile or so above sea level to get a sprat firmly in its beak, you will realise how remarkably short-sighted birds are. Not that the thread will be there for long; usually, on the very evening that the tapestry has been woven, the lady of the house stampedes clean through it in her wellies to pick a handful of the parsley up there in the shade at the very back, because she wants to make the cold brisket at least looking nice. She then says that some people who shall remain nameless seem to take a positive delight in trying to break other people's ankles by rigging up a sort of Colditz arrangement of trip-wires all over the place and what do some people think a garden is, a place where you can move around without risk of breaking every bone in your body, or a heavily defended advance outpost of the 2nd Para Regiment?

Small boys, especially those belonging to one's next-door neighbours (the Latin botanical name is *Juvenalia proximissimma*), are a pest easily identified by the persistent, often repeated cry of "Can we have our ball back, mister?" There are three ways of dealing with this: (a) feign deafness—not much use, really; all that happens is that the little horror, thinking the coast is clear, scales the wall and lands on the lupins in his bovver-boots; (b) throw back the ball, or preferably another harder ball, and wait hopefully for the crash of glass; and (c) ask the pest to come round the front and through the house to retrieve his own blasted ball, and when within range, spray liberally with buckshot. (Note: owing to the interval between the cricket and football seasons having narrowed to a fortnight, and in some cases over-lapping, do not relax when junior next door stops pretending he's Boycott; in next to no time he'll be pretending he's Keegan, when of course the ball gets bigger, causes more damage to the ten-week stocks, and is harder to throw back.)

Gnomes, of course, cannot be classified as garden pests. They are harmless; they neither breed nor get at the lettuces nor require regular spraying with oxydemeton-methyl. They just stay put, grinning inanely even when the Russians send over all those hairy caterpillars. I must try to think of something nice to say about them.

M ary, Mary, cautious, chary,
How does your garden grow?
Through a permanent haze of aerosol sprays
And using this year such a lot of "Roseclear"
That everyone swears you've ICI shares
And with pesticides all in a row
And the mixture that's known as Bordeaux.

Mary, Mary, anxious, wary,
How does your garden thrive?
With BHC dust an absolute must
And you must now have tried every known
    fungicide
And time after time sloshed sulphur of lime
And formaldehyde on each chive
And the paraquat pongs on your drive.

Mary, Mary, apothecary,
The garden your grandmother grew
In her old-fashioned way knew only the spray
Of a watering-can before Man began
Exploiting the worth of good, honest earth
And Adam, of course, never knew
John Innes No 2.

Showing Round

— YOU WOULDN'T LIKE to see round the garden, would you?

— Well . . .

— Because, though I says it as shouldn't, it really is beginning to look rather nice. I mean, considering. And it's practically left off raining, I mean it's only a sort of drizzle, and you can borrow Arthur's wellies, they're bound to fit you, they're just about your size; only you mustn't get those divine new shoes—they're Gucci, aren't they? Well, they *look* Gucci, which I always think is what matters—you mustn't get them covered in mud, and the far end of the lawn where Arthur had the men in to fix the drainage is inclined to be a bit swampy and in any case now Arthur's developed this fetish for croquet he has a bit of a Thing about stiletto marks anywhere near his hoops. Now you're sure you want to?—or would you rather just stay here by the fire and have another gin? I mean, do *say*.

— Well . . .

— Good. Splendid. Super. We can go through this way and out the back; Arthur usually dumps his wellies in the cupboard under the stairs. You'd better slip on a cardie or something; we're rather exposed up here and when the wind's in the east or the north, or whatever it is, it's inclined to be breezy but of course madly healthy; if you're just getting over the flu it'll blow away all those cobwebs. Through here, dear—oops: I should have warned you, they *are* low, aren't they, the beams, and old Jacko in the village swears they're riddled with woodworm but both Arthur and I feel they give the place *character* and it's amazing how quickly one gets the knack of stooping automatically. That, of course, is typical: Arthur must have left his wellies in the toolshed, but not to worry, we can collect them on our way to the fruit-cage down at the foot of the garden through that gap in the hedge down there—you must have a grope through the fruit-cage, you never know, you might find a goosegog ripe enough to get your teeth into—only try not to walk on the grass, just stick to the crazy paving but dodge the cracks because we've just put in alyssum and aubrietia and Heaven knows how many different varieties of saxifrage and little miniature heathers and things, and we must give the poor darlings a chance. I'm sorry about the mess out here on the verandah, but last night Arthur was mixing peat with John Innes No 2 (you know, for potting up) and he had to do it here because it was absolutely *pelting* down, and *both* bags burst. You should have heard the language, *and* the woman who comes in from the village and "does" said she knew she was thought of as a sort of two-legged washing-machine but she'd no intention of starting up as a bulldozer as well, so perhaps on our way back from the fruit-cage you could hold one of those black plastic bags while I sweep up—or we could do it the other way round, because you don't really have to catch the 6.20, do you?

— Well...

— Of course you don't. Put your chiffon scarf over your head, dear, because your hair's getting blown all over the place and it looked so nice when you came off the train I hardly recognised you. Well, now, this, as if I needed to tell you, is the herbaceous border. We copied it exactly, clump for clump and plant for plant, from one of those chart things you see in the papers when the Ideal Home Exhibition's on, you know, with everything graded so the tall things like hollyhocks and red-hot pokers are at the back and the lupins and Michaelmas daisies and so on are in the middle and at the front you've all the small things like hellebore and Mrs Sinkin's pinks and whatever, giving what the gardening man in the *Mail* called "a carefully graduated bank-like effect of glorious summer-long colour". Only Arthur insisted on doing the whole thing one evening when he'd been to a Rotary lunch that had gone on a bit, so the red-hot pokers and the hollyhocks are down here at the front, but if you come a little further up here and kneel down and peer through all that digitalis there's the most gorgeous little clump of campanula right at the back there up against the wall. Careful,

dear—oops: you've stepped in it, I'm afraid that's
Bimbo—he's next-door's Great Dane and he's an
absolute poppet but sometimes I think they train
him to jump over the wall and do his jobs on this
side. Not to worry, when we get down to the veg
garden you can take a cabbage leaf or something
and it'll come off in a sec. Now *these*, as if again
you needed telling, are the rose-beds and if only
you'd come last week (it was Joyce Grenfell or
Ruth Draper or one of those people who used to
do other people who kept saying that, wasn't it?)
if only you'd come last week, well, one doesn't
want to boast, but they were an absolute *picture*,
but they've got a bit battered with all the gales
we've had these last few days. Arthur thought it
might be rather fun—you know what a sense of
humour he has—to have what he calls
"incompatible bedfellows", so across there
there's Fred Loads in the same bed as Minnehaha
and in the middle bed we've Ralph Tizard and
Wendy Cussons as cosy as cosy together and
here we've Grandpa Dickson, of all people,
bedded down with the Duchess of—*damn*: run,
dear, it'll only be a passing plump and we can
shelter in the toolshed, *no*, not across the grass,
dear, up that path and round through the veg,
there's a sort of beaten track between the runner
beans, only for Heaven's sake jump over the
marrows at the end of the row. Isn't it *maddening*,
Trev the Wev—he's the met man on Television
South, you don't get him in Town, you get that
sawn-off little one with the moustache, Trev the
Wev said occasional showers, sometimes heavy

and prolonged, spreading from the West and for
once he seems to have been right but, still, it's all
part of Life's rich tapestry and it *is* rather fun,
isn't it?

— Well...

— There we are: we made it. This is Arthur's pride
and joy, the toolshed, and where he's put those
wellies I cannot imagine, but it *is* rather snug,
isn't it? Arthur spends hours out here just sitting
thinking; he's not what you'd call a born
conversationalist, bless his cotton socks. Sit on
that bag of Chichester grit, dear, and if it's damp
put that old sacking under you; those up there
are the nails for Arthur's tools, you know, spade,
rake, hoe, fork, trowel, secateurs, and so on; and
those are Arthur's tools on the floor, spade, rake
hoe, fork, trowel, secateurs and what have you.
If you move nearer the door—d'you know, we've
been trying for months to get old Jacko from the
village to put in a new pane: that was Bimbo, or
rather Bimbo's ballie—but if you move nearer the
door you'll be out of the way of those drips from
the roof, though of course what you should have
done was grab Arthur's oil-skins when we were
hunting for those wellies in the cupboard under
the stairs, because that moiré silk twin-set is
absolutely divine but it's rather more Sloane
Square than Sussex, isn't it? No, panic ye not, it's
practically stopped; I'd a feeling in my water it'd
be one of those short sharp shock things that
Willie Whitelaw keeps on about, so let's press on
regardless with the conducted tour, shall we?

— Well...

— There you are, hardly raining at all, it's only drips from the trees. Through the gap in the hedge, dear, that's it to your left; it *was* quite a sizeable gap like Falaise or the one in Jilly Cooper's teeth, only Arthur keeps saying he'll get the shears out and never does, so the best thing is to go through it backwards and just keep nudging, it's perfectly all right, it's only privet. And *this*, as if you didn't know, is the fruit-cage which really is rather our pride and joy; I'll hold the netting up for you and you crawl under, just a minute, it's got caught in your hair, you'll have to crouch much lower, dear, because the netting's fixed on to these pole things to keep the sparrows out and mind you don't skid because you'd never believe it but Arthur put fresh straw down only three weeks ago but with all the rain we've been having it's gone a bit soggy. D'you know, we picked very nearly eleven pounds of rasps this year, you can see for yourself what a crop we had, all those rather indecent little white knob things where the fruit were, but of course if it's goosegogs you're after go for the lower branches right at the bottom of each bush, there's bound to be one or two if you just get right down on your—*Bimbo*! . . . now how in God's name did you get in? It's all right, dear, he only wants to be friendly, he may not look it but he's the soppiest date ever, if you tickle him under the chin he absolutely adores it and he'll lick you all over—Bimbo, *down*: she's a very dear friend of mine and we were at Roedean together and she's come all the way from Knightsbridge to spend a lovely day in the country—Bimbo, *no*, she's not playing hard to get, she just missed her footing and slipped backwards and there's no need to pin her down in the straw with those ridiculous great paw-paws—Bimbo, *scram*. Get the hell out of it. Honestly, if next-door wasn't on the Planning Committee and we weren't thinking of adding on a granny wing (where you'll always be welcome, dear) I think Arthur would write him one of his letters. You're all right, are you?

— Well . . .

— Next time you come down you really *must* wear slacks. Everyone does down here, we had the WI AGM in the Hall last Thursday and there wasn't a skirt in sight except the vicar, I don't mean he's at all that way, I mean he came to give the blessing in his cassock or hassock or whatever it's called. You did say you found loganberries too acid for your flatulence condition, didn't you, because there are two over here just starting to turn pink, however, not to worry, we'll get out by the escape route at the other end of the cage; I'll hold up the netting for you again, hang on a sec, you've your heel caught in it this time, never mind, dear, very good for the figure, all this stooping, get that tum of yours back to what it was in the Vth at Roedean. Well, now, *this*, which will come as no surprise to you, is the vegetable garden; take one of those rather droopy outside leaves off that cabbage, dear, and wipe your Guccis . . . it doesn't matter now? You are a sport. These are the peas: those early ones are over, this row is the middle crop which we're eating now, and those are the last sowing which aren't quite ready yet. Otherwise we could have given you some to take back to Knightsbridge. These *were* the early potatoes, they're called Ulster Chieftain and they're quite delicious, not a bit like Ian Paisley, but of course we finished them weeks ago; these are the Catrionas which we're having now; and *those* are the late ones— Desirée—which won't be ready for digging for at least another three weeks, otherwise you could have taken some of *them* back home with you. But I tell you what you *are* going to take back as un *p'tit souvenir du jardin*. D'you like chives?

— Well . . .

— You shall have a lovely clump of chives, by now they've masses of these rather attractive purple flowers all over them, remember to cut them off before you sprinkle the Vichysoisse, there you are, careful, it's rather damp, but you can wrap a tissue or something round the root and shove it in your handbag. Now if you can manoeuvre your way round the compost heap and I'll give you a hoist up over this heap, grass cuttings, dear, very good for manure mixed with rape and sewage sludge, and we'll go back through the gap in the hedge if we can find it and down to that other bed in the corner and I'm going to cut you an enormous armful of those gorgeous Madonna lilies. They're rather late this year but they've spread like mad and they all suddenly came out at the same time and we've so many we don't know how to get rid of them; if you *have* to catch the 6.20, after Haywards Heath it only stops at Gatwick and then all those Balhams and Claphams and Streathams and places, so if any football hooligans get in and see you looking rather pre-Raphaelite with that lovely delicate pale complexion of yours and all these lilies, you'll be perfectly safe, dear, sacrosanct, really. Hold them well away from you, dear, they're dripping a bit but we'll find an old copy of *Popular Gardening* to wrap them in. Oops ... it was a pigeon, dear. You know it's considered terribly lucky; it's on your shoulder, no, the other shoulder, don't rub it off in case you rub it in. Oh, well, take another leaf; not one of those, that's the magnolia stellata and rather special. Last August we were in the Dordogne and Arthur left the car under some trees outside the hotel we were staying in and in the morning you couldn't recognise the bonnet for droppings and you'll never believe this but he won fifteen francs in the *Loterie Nationale*. We had to go all the way back to Limoges to collect the money at the *tabac* where he'd bought the ticket; it cost a fortune in petrol but it does show you there's something in it. Bless you, dear; that's the fourth time you've sneezed since we came out of the toolshed; it's the pollen. You don't really have to catch the 6.20, do you, because it's almost six, isn't it amazing how the time flies when you're just meandering round a garden; because naturally I'd adore to run you to the station, only Tarquin's taking his latest steady, she's an absolute poppet but just the teensiest bit slanty-eyed, to a disco in Hurstpierpoint and I did say he could have the

43

car and he's in one of his parents-are-the-end moods, so you'll have to rush but you must come in and dry off in front of the fire and have another gin if there's time which I don't think there's going to be. We'll go in by the side door and do remember to duck, that's the idea, you see how quickly you get into the way of it—oops: yes, that's the other one, it's just a few inches lower than this one. Now that clock says five past, either it's fast and I'm slow or I'm slow and it's fast, but there's a short cut through Lady Hesketh's paddock, if you nip over the stile at the end of the lane and then go across the ploughed field when you get to the top of Poacher's Beacon you can see the station at the bottom of the hill on the other side. You didn't have a mack, did you, no, you said it was lovely and sunny in London, and you've got the chives and the Madonnas; Arthur—(I don't believe it: do you see what I see?... the wellies, on top of the telly)—Arthur will be livid at missing you, I warned him you were coming down but he's got this seminar thing in Ipswich and God knows when he'll get back. Now you will come back in the autumn, won't you, because though I says it as shouldn't the chrysanths are really out of this world and I really think in a place like this, with the sea fret drifting in and mixing with the low cloud over the Downs, the "season of mists and mellow fruitfulness" is the best time of the year and we can warn next-door because I know they'd love to show you round *their* garden after you've seen round ours again, theirs is *much* bigger than ours and all terraced, quite steep, really, and you can get to know Bimbo properly. I don't know why, but somehow I get the feeling that the way the pair of you hit it off in the fruit-cage, it's going to be the start of a beautiful friendship. So you will, won't you? I mean, you *promise—faithfully* . . .

— Well . . .

Don't come into the garden, Maud,
For the grass is overgrown
And the pollen count is set to mount
To a height as yet unknown.
There's a heavy dew which will soak you through
And it's much too wet to make love, my pet,
And the fierce Great Dane has slipped his chain
And is there at the gate, alone.

Don't come into the garden, Maud,
It's a total exclusion zone.
It's the sort of night when the midges bite
And the lilo's out on loan.
There's a rather strong and unusual pong
By that old ilex where we first had sex
And the two elm trees both have Dutch disease.
Just stay home, dear, but phone.

Don't come into the garden, Maud,
Where the grapes of wrath are sown.
Papa's in a rage for we ruined his sage
When last we two lay prone.
On the garden seat where we often meet
There are slimy trails which I think are snails
And the forecasts show there's a chance of
    snow—
You'd be frozen to the bone.

Don't come into the garden, Maud,
It's a visit you should postpone.
You've a delicate chest and I think it's best
If you just stay on your own.
The cesspool's in spate and those bats you hate
Are in rampant flight, so—some other night
Or perhaps not at all, for I'm having a ball
With your younger sister, Joan.

Coming to Terms

There is an odd theory, originated by the co-authors of *The Garden of Allah* and fostered by the compilers of seed catalogues, that a garden is primarily a place in which to enjoy oneself and feel at peace with the world. Even when few parts of the world are at peace with themselves or with each other. If you take a sheet of paper and set down in one column the hours spent per annum leaning back and thinking how lovely the garden's looking after that overnight rain, and in another column the hours per annum spent in trying to make it look lovely, you will realise that the argument is not without its flaws. The ratio between the two sets of figures is roughly that of a nurse's average take-home pay put alongside the combined national debts of Argentina, Poland, and Chelsea: the Football Club, not the Flower Show.

Gardening is *not* a recreational pursuit; you may get a kick out of it, but if you stick to the rules you should also get a rick, usually down at the bottom end of the vertebrae, just above the coccyx, after digging the trench for the new asparagus bed. When you get down to it, as sooner or later you must, gardening is a long-drawn-out war of attrition against the elements, a tripartite agreement involving the animal, insect and bird worlds, and the occasional sheer perversity of Nature. Tell me, if you will, using the other side of the paper on which you reckoned up those hours per annum, why it is that a single seed blown by a gust of wind or dropped from some gormandising starling's over-stuffed beak can cover the rubble on a bomb site or the most unsightly railway embankment with a gloriously patterned quilt of foxgloves without any outside assistance ... when some precious cutting, hormoned and carefully groomed, planted at just the right time in just the right place and just the right soil and cosseted like a new-born babe, refuses to "take".

This is what we're up against, and it is by no means all. In her day, the mother of the lady of the house was an acknowledged doyenne of the cliché; she came out in clichés the way other people come out in spots or rashes. Her daughter fell heir to most of the maternal anthology, and over the years has added a few of her own. They include such nuggets of wisdom as, you can only take out what you put in, if you just sit waiting for it to happen it'll never happen, and things are only good in the long run if they've been properly looked after at the start.

What is so infuriating about these little gems, especially when repeated like a favourite long-playing cassette, is that there is no really effective come-back. A couple of years ago, the Wimbledon authorities bought some company's disused sports ground within lobbing distance of their own hallowed turf. The committee was getting a little irked by complaints from the players about the lack of practice facilities on grass; the players said that while they

49

didn't mind Billie-Jean bouncing all over the place at her advanced age, it took them time to get used to the balls behaving in the same way, especially on Court No 2. A triumvirate of Wimbledon's most experienced groundsmen was packed off to the outback to see what could be done with the former playing-fields, where the grass was waist-high. By the start of the 1982 championships there were a dozen or more practice courts smooth enough and fast enough to satisfy even Lendl, the sulky Czech who maintains that grass is meant only for cows, no slight intended on the Ladies' Singles entrants.

The relevant but depressing fact in this incident is that the leading groundsman, interviewed on how the miracle had been achieved, said: "*Work*. All there is to it: hard work. We mowed and we rolled and we sowed, and we kept on mowing and rolling and sowing, and then we mowed a lot more and rolled a helluva lot more and just kept at it, rolling and rolling and mowing and sowing. And rolling. Only way to get results: *work*. Hard work. Bloody hard work. Nothing to it."

I could have killed him. The lady of the house read the interview first and came out with, you know what my dear old mother used to say, God rest her soul—even if it's only a plain ordinary steak and kidney pudding, for every mouthful that goes down you there's been a solid twenty minutes of thought and loving care and honest sweat gone into it, as well as two kidneys. So here is a brief glossary of horticultural terms covering a few of the tasks which help to fill in the eight thousand, seven hundred and fifty-seven hours in the gardener's year (eight thousand, seven hundred and seventy-one in Leap Year) and still leave the remaining three hours per annum completely free for leaning back and thinking how lovely it's looking after the overnight rain.

Advising   A surprising amount of a gardener's life is taken up with either advising or receiving advice from other gardeners. Usually the amount received greatly exceeds the amount given; the few times I presume to proffer, the reaction is "You're a fine one to talk, what about your parsnips last year?" Disregard *all* advice, except when someone says if you're really thinking of digging up and dividing all those old clumps of irises, he'll come round and show you how. Ask him round at once, and say while he's getting on with it you'll nip indoors and see if there's a lager in the fridge for him when he's finished. Tell him if there isn't, you'll nip round to the pub and get him one, and it's no trouble.

Bending   Homo sapiens, with a few exceptions like Richard III, is a fairly erect species; gardeners, however, spend much of their lives curved, like the human hoops in the *Alice in Wonderland* game of croquet, but purpler. Life would have been a lot easier for us had we been built on the lines, say, of the Himalayan brown bear who at least can stand up straight on its back paws when trimming the hedge and then get back down on all fours for weeding. If you hear a click on your way down, your cervicle processes need re-processing; if there's a louder click when you try to get back up again, your subcutaneous acromium is out of sync. If you kid yourself you're so fit you never feel so much as a

twinge when bending, you're bent.

Clearing Up   There are few things more satisfying, after hours of weeding, pruning, thinning-out, dead-heading, etc., (all of which *q.v.*) than sweeping up the mess into one large, impressive heap. There are few things less satisfying, especially in a small town garden, than trying to get rid of the damn stuff. Bribe the dustmen? No longer: refuse disposal executives are now under orders from NUPE to refuse even a fallen forget-me-not petal. Bonfire? Too damp; anyway, wind variable, and complaints from neighbours about smalls hung on line covered in smuts. Move mess and add to compost heap? Pointless, really; might as well move compost heap and add to mess. Better leave clearing up to lady of house. You never know, if you promise her a nice run in the car to see the rhododendrons at Petworth, she *might*.

Digging   Here I have to declare a personal interest, or lack of interest. Early in the 1914–18 war my mother, after accompanying Dame Clara Butt singing "Land of Hope and Glory" in the Corn Exchange, Berwick-upon-Tweed, became excessively patriotic and had all the back garden and the front lawn taken up to Dig for Victory. As a result—though I realize it's something that has got to be done, like remembering to take off your gardening boots before sitting down to watch *Crossroads*—I do not dig digging. It's an unrewarding role; you don't catch Paul Schofield playing even the First Gravedigger in *Hamlet*. Though the interment technique can help: grasp the spade firmly and imagine you are preparing the ground for a few people you think might be better under it—Castro, say, or the Ayatollah Khomeinni, or the little man in the off-license who never has change for a tenner—and start digging. You'll be surprised.

Earthing Up Sometimes known as *blanching*, *cf.*, "... as Tarquin's sapphire-blue eyes pierced her heaving bosoms, Deborah blanched visibly..." (Barbara Cartland). The theory is that celery and chicory need earthing up to keep the light out of their eyes and make them look pale and uninteresting when served. The odd thing about the theory is that leeks do *not* need earthing up, but still manage to look pale and uninteresting when served and have a great deal more taste than chicory.

Forking This is a more fragmented form of digging, recommended when taking up potatoes. If you use a spade, you can be sure that at least one potato will be cleft in twain; by using a fork, all that happens is that two or at the most three of the prongs will go clean through the potato. Whichever method is adopted, serve mashed.

Grafting Don't attempt it. Leave it to the experts: it's the gardening equivalent of artificial insemination, donors welcome, and you wouldn't like to take on that Mr Steptoe's job, would you? Just go on reading the advertisements: *NEW*! ... Your Own Fruit Salad on a Single Fast-Growing Guaranteed Trouble-Free Tree!! ... Golden Delicious Apples, Victoria Plums, and Conference Pears—ALL THREE in Staggering Profusion on the Same Branch!!! ... Order your sensational new PLUMPPLEPEAR *NOW* while stocks last!!!! People do, too. (See *Suckers*.)

Hoeing   God, there's no end to it, is there? The hoe is a tool designed to obviate backache (see *Bending*). You jab or scratch or scrape away in the small places between the asters, and in doing so either sever or uproot the asters. You then get down on your knees to replant them or pick up the bits. It would have been simpler to have got down on your knees in the first place and got the groundsel out by hand.

Irrigation   With all the rain we had last fortnight? *Joking*, you gotta be.

Kitchen Gardening   Well, now, take mange-tout. You know we got very nearly a pound-and-a-quarter of mange-tout off that one row? I mean, work it out for yourself: the seed cost 75p the packet, say seventy-two hours sowing, fixing all that black thread over them for the bloody birds, staking them, watering, chucking out the ones that got foot rot, spraying the ones that were left with BHC in case of weevils, re-staking them after the gales we had in June, and then picking them; seventy-two hours even at the daily woman's minimum two quid an hour, that's £144. And we got enough for when the in-laws came for Sunday lunch, well, eked out with mashed swedes and broccoli. It works out at somewhere around £4.80 a pod. But that's not the point. The point is that we grew them ourselves, and they taste a damn sight better than any of that shop stuff. I mean, what are they charging now for a tin of processed peas in Sainsbury's? 13p? 14p, even? (Both the lady of the house and I rather like processed peas, but we would never dream of giving up the vegetable garden. I mean, it makes sense, doesn't it, growing your own stuff and knowing it's fresh and saving all that money. Look how well Richard Briers has done since he was in *The Good Life*.)

The rest of the alphabet—A–Z—will be dealt with later. Meantime, I am going indoors to pour out a large Scotch. There will be no danger of yet another gardening error. Over-watering.

Sheds
(Like, for example, Fred's
At the foot of his allotment)
Are not meant
To be architecturally admired
Nor are they required
To conform to any conventional design.
They can, in fact, combine
The neo-Gothic with the Victorian era
Or, coming a little nearer,
The shanty-town technique with the
   Impressionist
Or those small religious cubicles patronised by
   the confessionist
With the sort of buildings Heath Robinson drew
Or an outside loo.

Fred's shed
Is not what you would call symmetrical. Instead,
Half-hidden in a tangle
Of dockens and nettles, it has no right angle.
It lurches precariously to starboard
And its roof, of once-tarred hardboard,
Flaps impatiently in a gale.
The door, bought years ago in a sale
Of do-it-yourself rejects, either sticks
Or is held in position by bricks.

It would never enter Fred's head
To get rid of the shed.
In it are the tools of his trade:
His rake, his hoe, his fork, his spade;
A great many broken pots,
A great deal of garden twine in knots;
A small primus stove on which to brew a cupper
To keep him going until he gets home for supper;

On one wall, an old pin-up calendar by Pirelli;
In one corner, for some unexplained reason, a
    single wellie;
And, keeping cool under an upturned pail,
Two pint bottles of brown ale.
And here Fred sits, contentedly drinking,
Smoking his pipe, and thinking
How people dream of their Shangri la-di-dahs
And houses with swimming pools and posh
    foreign cars
And none of them gets half the pleasure, when
    all's done and said
As he does on his own in this ramshackle old
    shed.

An Englishman's home is his castle, he read.
No castle was ever as homely to Fred
As his shed.

. . . by any other name . . .

"IT'S SWEET WILLIAM!" screamed a tabloid. *Dianthus barbatus*, it might have added, except that neither is a really suitable name for a future monarch. This was way back in June, '82, shortly after the arrival of the eventual heir to the throne, when for days Ladbrokes and the rest of the nation had been speculating on what he would be called. I was sitting out in the garden (it was that fine evening in the middle of the month, if you remember, just before the heavens performed their ritual opening ceremony in time for Wimbledon and the second Test), thinking not about the baby's names but about the extraordinary ones given to most of the plants and shrubs and even the weeds all around me.

Who chooses them, d'you suppose? Who decides? Who slipped the crumpled-up last-minute note to the vicar just before Amaranthus, say, was christened tipping him off that the new variety was also to be known as Love Lies Bleeding *and* Joseph's Coat? I can understand the first alternative; Amaranthus looks, I suppose, how love might look when bleeding: it's red and it droops. It's not at all my idea of Joseph's coat which, if I've read my Old Testament correctly, skipping bits of Habakkuk and all of Micah, was psychodelic. Even, as Andrew Lloyd Webber found to his financial gain, technicoloured. Was it the parents or the godparents who insisted on calling spurge Euphorbia? I see their point. It must be awful to go through life being introduced at parties with the hostess saying, "I don't think you've met Spurge, have you?" Much better to start off the evening with "No need to tell any of you who *this* is—yes, it's Euphorbia, whom you've heard us talk so much about."

Naming either plants or humans in advance, not knowing how they're going to turn out, is tricky; so many new varieties of either look much the same, rather old and wrinkly. A girl christened Rose may develop into a proper little snapdragon; a Baby Blue Eyes (her real name is Nemophila) can end up a Black-Eyed Susan (she'll be Thunbergia on her passport when she's old enough to have one). The last soprano I saw playing Little Buttercup with the d'Oyly Carte Opera Company looked more a fully-blown paeony to me.

I can understand the botanist who has discovered some new species getting a bit big-headed and insisting on it being named after himself or herself. One of mankind's greatest benefactors was a botanist called Lawson who in the middle of the nineteenth century in the forests of Oregon hit on the evergreen known (not often, and never after a couple of drinks) as *Chamaecyparis lawsoniana*, and if ever a man deserved to have his name immortalised he did. It, the *C. lawsoniana*, forms just about the fastest-growing hedge ever, sometimes, if you egg it on, achieving a growth of between three and four feet per annum; next to a very tall brick wall, which requires planning permission, it is by far the best thing on the market to stop next-door leaning over and saying you do know, don't you, that the trouble with those tomatoes of yours is botrytis and what you want to do if they're not too far gone is fumigate them with tecrazene.

I bless the name of Lawson every year as the results of his ferreting around on his hands and knees all over Oregon grow steadily taller and thicker and more impenetrable. Once a thwarted voyeur—the kind who stops and stares when you're weeding the front garden wearing those old shorts with the zip-fastener trouble—was heard muttering on the other side of the Iron Curtain "Wot d'you s'pose goes on be'ind all that 'edge, eh?" "Orgies, I shouldn't be surprised," said his companion. "'E looks the type. Anyway, no-one would grow an 'edge that thick unless they'd somethin' to 'ide." There was a certain amount of truth in the supposition, even if in my case all that might have needed a good hiding would have been due to a slip of the zip. And you could hardly call that an orgy. Well, no-one has done so up to now.

The common names of some plants—not many—at least give you an idea of what they're going to look like when they grow up, if they ever do. Bachelor's Buttons look like buttons; kerria, their proper name, sounds something you'd shy away from or perhaps an Italian half-back, which amounts to the same thing. With a bit of imagination, the shrimp plant looks like a shrimp; its other name, beloperone, sounds like someone in Greek mythology. Tell anyone you'd like to show them your physalis and they edge away to the far end of the sofa and say they'd no idea how late it was; ask them to come and admire your Chinese Lanterns, and there's no trouble at all.

I can understand why the sansevieria is called Mother-in-Law's Tongue—Heaven knows it's sharp enough and pointed—but calling a modest unassuming little thing like the helxine Mind-Your-Own-Business seems unfair. The kniphofia *looks* like a red-hot poker, or at least like the dummy ones wielded by clowns in old-fashioned harlequinades; why the acalyphus, which strikes me as a calm, cool and collected, rather elegant plant, should be called a Red-Hot Cat-Tail is a bafflement. Who was the Livingstone after whom the Livingstone daisy was named? The Doctor, I presume. It couldn't have been Ken, who mercifully wouldn't have been around at the time. Whoever it was, there was a valid reason for giving it an ordinary name: its proper one is mesembryanthemum, and no-one wants to spend a lifetime trying to pronounce that sort of thing, let alone trying to spell it.

Just as parents regret saddling their young with names which prove unsuitable later in life—like Patience or Christian or Gay—some plants seem to have been treated thoughtlessly at the font. They're all delightful species, but if you say that your fatsia is next to your fleabane, the turtlehead is crowding out your streptocarpus, and you'll have to thin out your lavatera to get a glimpse of your Gardener's Garters, it doesn't sound a bit nice. Apart from Butcher's Broom (I get this picture of some member of the Dewhurst family sweeping up lights in the sawdust) most common names sound better than the official ones. Beauty Bush sounds better than kolkwitzia; Bird of Paradise flower better than strelitzia; Star of Bethlehem infinitely preferable to ornithogalum. This is particularly true, mentioning Star of Bethlehem, in religious gardening circles. If I say that under my Candles of the Lord is Solomon's Seal and my Temple Bells are within pealing range of Rose of Sharon, it at least sounds more C of E than saying the polygonatum's under the yucca and the smithiantha's not too far from the hypericum.

Sometimes, though, the Latin botanical name is dead right. I used to waste hours solving, or trying to solve, the *Guardian* crossword. The arch-sadist among the setters of these puzzles trades under the pseudonym Araucaria. Because he included far too many classical allusions for my liking, I took him in my ignorance to be a lesser-known Roman emperor or at least a centurion on the make. One day, maddened by the clue for 23 across: "you can't win unless you toughen vintner, confused" (it turned out to be an anagram of "nothing venture"), I looked him up and found that Araucaria was the U-name for the monkey puzzle tree. Very apt; very subtle; one up to Araucaria: he'd had me puzzling since shortly after lunch and certainly made a monkey out of me. I switched to the junior crossword in the *Express*.

One of the odd things about the names of plants is that so many of them sound like the diseases the plants are liable to catch. They're really interchangeable. When you're showing someone round the garden and they ask what's the name of

that thing over there in the corner with the attractive little blue flower, if you say firmly "Amnesia" the chances are that the come-back will be "Of *course*, stupid of me, Mother used to have it up in Northamptonshire." I have an occasional flight of fancy in which a hypochondriac gardener goes to consult a horticulturally-minded GP . . .

— Well, now, Mrs Liverwort, what's the trouble, eh? Touch of the old plumbago again?

— No, doctor, it's not that. I think it's me coleus. If it isn't me coleus, it's me corylopsis. I get these twinges, right up me fritillaria.

— Just lie down on the couch-grass and we'll run the mower over you. How's your appetite—getting enough humus, are you? Nasty cough, that: I'd prune back on the nicotiana, if I were you. Show me your hound's tongue, please . . . m'm: slight uvularia, but nothing the matter with your epidendrum. Everything regular where the lavatera's concerned, is it?

— Oh, yes, doctor. But I've this lump here. You don't think it's calceolaria, do you?

— *That*? No, no, that's either a small rhizome or a cistus; nothing to worry about. Take a deep breath, please, and say "Amaryllis" . . . uh-huh: d'you have any trouble with your salvia?

— Only when I propagate, doctor. I get these bouts of nemesia, all round me pergola.

— Boron deficiency: soon put that right. You're very lucky, y'know, for a mature growth like yourself . . . no wistaria, not a sign of schizanthus trouble, and your oleanders are in perfect

65

condition. Slight touch of stephanotis and you want to watch that buddleia of yours—I'll give you this prescription, couple of bergamots and a berberis three times a day, and if you spray that ribwort of yours with pyrethrum you'll be as right as a privet in no time. There you are: take that to your nearest nurseries and they'll mulch it up for you.

— You don't think, doctor, a fortnight in a conservatory?

— Mrs Liverwort, this is the National Health Service. Not the Royal Horticultural Society.

Another odd thing is that so many weeds which you'd expect to have unattractive names have charming ones. Trefoil and cinquefoil; celandine and speedwell; shepherd's purse and woodrush. But a rose, as Gertrude Stein might have written and probably did if only to fill up space, is a rose is a rose is a rose. Juliet, when she advanced the theory that they would smell as sweet by any other name, wasn't to know that in the fulness of time they would be given names like Whisky Mac and Peek-a-Boo and Chinatown and Anna Ford. But the girl was absolutely right; roses, or most of them, would smell as sweet even if called Jonathan Dimbleby or HM Collector of Taxes. And not only roses. The fragrance of *Allium sativum* lingers on every bit as long and as lovingly when you call it garlic.

There is a legend in Babylon
    where people are inclined to gabble on
that the hanging gardens
were jardins
created by a sort of superior
version of Percy Thrower called Nazir-el-Kish of
    Sumeria
with the idea that everything would dangle
downwards at an attractive angle

but until Babylonia discovered irrigation
the sun in that unfortunate nation
was so strong and so bright
that everything stayed upright
and refused to droop
which left Nazir-el-Kish not only in the soup
but redundant and on the shelf

so he hanged himself.

Veg

I KNEW A gardener once—a devout but eccentric Anglican—who mumble-mumbled his way through the Benedicite until it came to "O all ye Green Things upon the Earth, bless ye the Lord" when he fairly let rip. Green Things to him were much more important than ye Whales, and all that move in the Waters; more important, even, than Ananias, Azarias, and Misael who have always seemed an odd trio to be included in a general summons to do homage to the Almighty. Rather like finding Wilson, Keppel and Betty tacked on to a roll-call of the twelve Apostles. My friend got into trouble once with the Creed; while the rest of the congregation continued with the orthodox version after the opening words "I believe", he was heard one Sabbath morning intoning "for every drop of rain that falls, a flower grows".

But green things rather than floral displays were what mattered to him; he paid a great deal more attention to his vegetable garden than to his rose-beds, his argument being that by and large roses could look after themselves and celery couldn't. He lived to an over-ripe old age, becoming in appearance more and more like the beetroot he cultivated so expertly, and to his dying day maintained that—if the law hadn't been such an ass—finding any tinned vegetable in a larder ought to count as grounds for divorce.

Veg apart, there's much to be said for having a vegetable garden, however small. There's the rather endearing fantasy that growing your own veg works out at around one-tenth of the cost of buying them (for explosion of myth, see para on mange-tout in "Kitchen Gardening" earlier in this volume). There's the old oneupmanship ploy again . . . well, of course, we grow all our own; we had ratatouille last night and everything in it—aubergines, marrow, courgettes, tomatoes, peppers, even the bay leaf, but *everything*— came out of the garden or the greenhouse; Jennifer, bless her little cotton socks, had *three* helpings and then was sick all over the sealyham and either on or over the can the whole night and Dr Chapman thinks she has some sort of aubergine allergy.

There's the theory—undeniable, really—that your own veg taste better than the ones in the shops, not surprising considering the way the ones in the shops are manhandled by the customers. The first new potatoes, freshly dug out of your own back garden, not peeled, not even scrubbed, just given a wipe with your thumb and popped into the pan and dished up with a sprig of mint and a dollop of butter . . . they have that wonderful earthy taste, even when small bits of terra firma get under your plate and you have to excuse yourself from the dining-table and nip upstairs for a quick rinse.

The one drawback about a vegetable garden is that it needs looking after. Here is a handy, practical month-by-month reminder of just a few—by no means all—of the essential tasks to be carried out if you want your choice of veg to be more than the usual watery cabbage and/or stringy runner beans. Cut it out and paste it on the inside of the door of your fridge, where you keep the frozen peas, the cans of imported Israeli new potatoes, and the cellophane-wrapped deep-freeze Californian sweet corn.

January Complete digging started in December and held up by festive season, visit of in-laws, annual repeat of *Gone With The Wind* on TV, and Boxing Day indigestion. *Order* seed potatoes and arrange in trays, covering with newspaper, in the hope that they'll start sprouting those rather suggestive little pink things at the end opposite the one you'd expected. *Study* seed catalogues, preferably in front of blazing log fire and with a large Scotch within reach; decide as in previous years not to bother with artichokes, chicory, or parsnips (too much trouble, and in case of last-named lady of house's Boxing Day indigestion apt to continue until March at earliest); decide to grow more cress, perhaps three pkts to be sown to provide rotation of crops. *Sow* early broccoli. *Buy* Algerian lettuce (Sainsbury's), Tanzanian broad beans (Waitrose), and out-of-season South African spring onions (Marks and Sparks). *Harvest* broccoli.

February Complete digging held up by ground too hard due to frost, ground too soggy due to floods, meeting with accountants re bills due to gas, electricity, rating authority and Collector of Taxes, and torture return visit to in-laws. *Sow* more early broccoli under glass. *Check* seed potatoes in trays: no sign of suggestive little pink things, but interesting article on C P Snow's private life in old copy of *S Times* covering trays; sit on dampish sack of John Innes in greenhouse and read. *Buy* newly-arrived Catalonian leeks (British Home Stores), out-of-season Provençal melons (Fortnum's), and three pkts cress (shop round corner). *Harvest* broccoli.

March Complete digging. Start hoeing. If soil workable, *sow* peas, beans, carrots, leeks, radishes, summer spinach and patch on gardening trousers where split after stooping to count number of slugs trapped in upturned semi-grapefruit (none: this year's slugs obviously anti-citrus). If soil not workable, stay indoors and listen to *Gardeners' Question Time*, muttering things like "Well, even I could have told them *that*." Also *sow* middle crop broccoli and first rotation of cress. *Prepare* asparagus bed, then fill in and buy expensive bunch of Florida asparagus as treat for lady of house's birthday, having forgotten card. *Transplant* onions to permanent position, at the same time uprooting chives mistaking same for non-flowering muscari with no right in veg garden. *Harvest* broccoli.

April Keep hoeing. *Prepare* celery bed; then see freshly-imported, crisp, perfectly blanched Zimbabwean celery in Tesco's; buy large bunch and fill in bed. *Sow* late broccoli. Remember seed potatoes in trays covered by old copy of *S Times*; suggestive little pink things now rather sinister weirdly-shaped tentacles, but interesting article by A J P Taylor on back of C P Snow's private life; read same while deciding whether worth while planting out tentacled tubers. Decide against; first supplies of Jersey new potatoes now available in International Stores, and anyway thinking of going on F-for-fibre diet and cutting down on carbohydrates.

Sow peas, beans, kale, turnips, and late season broccoli. Also *sow* second rotation cress, next-door cat having fouled first rotation when greenhouse door left open overnight during potential mating season. *Harvest* broccoli. Ignore lady of house's rather laboured attempts at sarcasm in saying (a) there's a limit to the number of ways even Robert Carrier could serve up bloody broccoli, and (b) small wonder Paul McCartney is suing left, right and centre when you think that the Beatles made films for a producer with a name like *that*.

May Complete hoeing. Start raking. Watch neighbours earthing up potatoes and calculate amount of time and labour saved by not planting tuberous tentacles. *Pot up* on shelf in greenhouse "Pixie" tomatoes (bush type, require no staking). Towards end of month, stake "Pixies" owing to greenhouse door being left open in gale. *Sow under glass* marrows (early May) and cucumbers (late May), wondering if it's the other way round but unable to check as gardening encyclopedia borrowed in 1979 by you can't remember whom, but think it was Mr Handyside in No 38 who joined Mormons and emigrated to Utah.

Plant out next season's early broccoli, and *harvest* last of this season's late broccoli, avoiding lady of house during operation. *Buy* just-arrived Italian endives (M and S), newly-imported Tanzanian savoys (Co-op), and Jerusalem artichokes (7fr in

Dieppe market, cheap day trip from Newhaven, cost including excellent lunch for two approx. £80, heavy swell all the way back and artichokes inadvertently left on seat in Normandy bar on ss *Senlac*).

June Remove cloches from marrows and cucumbers around June 6th in time for surprise late night frost on June 7th. *Plant out* more broccoli just in case, and *sow* third cress rotation, second having been wiped out by dachshund jumping up on greenhouse staging in attempt to sort things out once and for all with next-door cat. *Re-stake* "Pixies", as dachshund and next-door car obviously did complete circuit(s) of greenhouse in sorting-out process. *Buy* tinned Normandy petit pois (Fine Fare), Lithuanian frozen brassica (Kwiksave), and Smash (shop round corner). Relatively slack month, really; spring broccoli over and winter broccoli not yet ready, so no broccoli harvesting. Lady of house much more amiable.

July *Earth up* brussels sprouts; or, better still, if sprouts bought in supermarket just undo cellophane wrapping and boil for approx. 10 mins in slightly salted water with the lid on. *Check* courgettes for foot rot and onions for eelworm and mildew; after checking, abandon plans for laying down enough ratatouille in deep-freeze to see through winter. Make room for swedes; also (especially in buses) Danes, Norwegians and other Scandinavian students over here to learn English at disco late-nite raves. No broccoli harvesting. Lady of house positively affable; obviously looking forward to holidays.

August Holidays. Relatives, friends, neighbours, etc, *harvest* peas, beans, spinach, calabrese, marrows,

cucumbers, onions, lettuces, "Pixies" galore, etc, etc; and then have the nerve to expect a souvenir of Lesbos in return for "keeping an eye on things".

September   *Dig up and burn* ravaged and podless pea- and bean-stalks; *up-stake* "Pixies", tie up stakes neatly and store for next year, then *destroy* withered and barren remnants of plants. Rake over beds where the lettuces and radishes were before you went away. Start reading first of seed catalogues; make note to order seed potatoes earlier this time, also more broccoli and cress.

October/November Start digging. *Harvest* first of winter broccoli.

December Continue digging. *Prepare* beds for in-laws. *Buy* new line of imported Kuwaitan shallots (Alliance Cash and Carry), deep-freeze Canadian chicory (Tesco's), and—strange how quickly the seasons come round when you've a vegetable garden—*two* bunches Florida asparagus (Fortnum's) as special Christmas treat before in-laws arrive. Carry on digging. See osteopath re back. *Harvest* broccoli.

And throughout the year think of the money you're saving, the exercise you're getting pushing trolleys round supermarkets, and the good all that roughage is doing you.

Down by the salley gardens my love and I did
  meet
And she did polite "beg pardons" after what she
  found to eat.
In the radish bed she fed and fed and my slender
  garden fence
Was bowed in the wind while the neighbours
  grinned at my loved one's flatulence.

Down by the salley gardens my love and I did
  stand
And she scoffed the lot in the spring onion plot
  'til it all got out of hand;
For a garden, be it humble, seems an awesome
  storm-tossed thing
When your loved one starts to rumble and you
  sense the breath of Spring.

Down by the salley gardens my love and I did
  part
For the heart that's tender hardens when
  digestive troubles start.
She ate parsnips raw and at last I saw how
  dyspepsia usurps
The tranquil calm of a loved one's charm, and I
  left her with her burps.

Herbs

— AND TELL ME, Ms Herbison, how did you get *into* herbs?
— I told you. When we were rehearsing what to say off the cuff.
— Er, I'll switch off and re-wind. (*This is the take, dammit.*) Ready?
— Naturally.
— And tell me, Ms Herbison, how did you get *into* herbs?
— Well, Evelyn, my common law husband, and I had this sudden urge to Get Away From It All. You know, from pollution and Roy Hattersley and being on the *Readers' Digest* mailing list, all that sort of thing. We felt we'd reached what Evelyn called thatcheration point. So we got an Arts Council grant and bought this disused barn and the plot of land up here in Cumbria (Russell Harty's uncle is our nearest neighbour, but as we don't have television and he's carnivorous we have very little in common) and it all began in a very small way—little jars of homemade mint sauce for Age Concern, personally-embroidered sachets of parsley tea for the Mothers' Union ...

you know parsley tea is an absolute must for inducing labour in difficult cases?
— Really?
— But yes. So it goes like a bomb with the MU. I don't mean the musicians, they couldn't care less, I mean the mothers. Then we took a stall in Penrith market, and from then on the whole thing just topsy'd. Now we have our own flourishing mail-order business, Mrs Herbison's Home-Grown Herbs (I put the r back in Mrs because Evelyn was writing at the time and he hated anything coming back through the post with ms on it) with a world-wide herbal clientele, some of it quite famous. President Reagan keeps needing a great deal of balm (rue, too, sometimes, but not often), Tony Benn gets madder every month, Dr Runcie has his standing order for monkshood, and all David Steel seems to think he needs is thyme.
— But, surely, your herbs are used mainly in the kitchen—I mean, for flavouring casseroles and stews and—
— Well, now, if and when this ever goes out on *Woman's Hour* or *Kaleidoscope* or whatever, that is a popular misconception which I would like to crush in the same way that I crush juniper stalks, caraway seeds, and the stigmas of saffron. Abysmally few people realise that herbs are bi-functional. They have their culinary uses, certainly; but their therapeutic qualities are woefully under-estimated. Here: taste that.
— Well . . .
— Go on: taste. Take a good mouthful and swallow.

What's the verdict?

— Yuk.

— Yes, it has a pleasantly aromatic bitter taste. That is hyssop. Now a little hyssop added to soups or salads, or the leaves finely chopped up and sprinkled over a tart—delicious. But do you ever pause to think, while munching a hyssop-sprinkled tart, that hyssop contains flavonoid glycoside, which is an absolute *sine qua non* for inhibiting the secretion of the sweat glands? You add it to, say, chicken broth; fair enough, it takes away the taste of the chicken; but it is also the cat's pyjamas in easing spasms in digestive upsets, it's very good as a gargle, and the French add it to absinthe, with of course wormwood.

— And gall?

— Southern France, mainly. Oh; I see what you mean. It was a play on words. Hardly up to Shavian standards, or even Pinero. Radio 4 rather than 3, really. However. Taste that.

— Well...

— Go on: taste. Roll it round the palate and gurgitate. Well?

— Ugh.

— That is dill. Ordinary, common-or-garden dill; or, to be more precise, the oil obtained from crushed dill-tops. And, as of course you know, dill adds its own distinctive flavour to sauces, fish dishes, anything eggy on a tray, and it's excellent for pickling when vinegarised. But what you didn't know, I'll be bound, is that it *not only relieves flatulence but also increases lactation.* So the next time you're full of wind but short on

milk, there's your answer: dill. Try this one.
— Honestly, I had lunch in the BH canteen . . .
— Go on: try it. Marjoram. Very good for stuffing, you can put the leaves in a salad, or chop them up and sprinkle them over lamb or pork or veal if you're foolish enough to eat such things. But what is much more important is the fact that dill acts as an intestinal antispasmodic; you simply cannot beat it for stimulating the bile. It's also very good for colic and diarrhoea and putting in salami. Have a go at this one.
— Really, I . . .
— On you go: it's perfectly safe unless taken during pregnancy. That's crushed tarragon. No, it isn't; the labels must have got mixed. It's crushed rosemary. I had a great-aunt who was an actress with Sir Frank Benson's Shakespearean Company; she got her big chance as Ophelia in Dundee, but in the mad scene she couldn't for the life of her remember what rosemary was for. So she was fired, first by ambition, and then by Benson. But I digress. People think of rosemary as adding a sort of panache to lamb or looking nice in fruit cup; taken either internally as an infusion or applied externally as an ointment, you'd be surprised at the things it can do for you. Increases the urine flow, alleviates rheumatism, acts as an insect repellent. No-one who has rheumatism, wasps, and trouble in going should ever be without it. 95p the small-size tub, p and p extra. I forgot: it's the Beeb, no advertising except Benson and Hedges round the edges at Old Trafford. Now I can see by the expression on

your face that what you're dying to ask next is how we prepare our herbs before they're put on the market . . .

— Actually, I was . . .

— So I'll tell you. They're all spread out to dry here on the barn floor, which is perfectly clean now we've got rid of the goat. Then the stalks and the stigmae and in some cases the roots are crushed and the male and female flower-heads segregated, and all the shucks and bits and pieces which have dropped on the floor get swept up and put in those little muslin bags as *bouquets garnis*. After all, no-one has the foggiest idea what's in a *bouquet garni* unless one gets inadvertently left in an Irish stew and swallowed, and even then all it tastes of is wet muslin. Then the dried herbs are put in their jars or pots or in empty yoghourt cartons (in our busy season, Lent, we get through a great deal of yoghourt) and labelled, trying to remember what's in what and not getting the labels mixed up. Then it's just a matter of letting President Reagan have his balm and Ted Heath his crushed European hellebore, and supplying the rest of the clientele.

— You must have a very wide selection of herbs?

— You can see for yourself: all those jars, it's like Ali Baba and the Forty Thieves. I think we've everything a *cordon bleu* chef might require—if he's a hypochondriac, too, that is: coltsfoot (seasoning soups and alleviating varicose veins); savory (equally good for flavouring sausages and relieving catarrh); horehound (adds bite to dandelion soup and works wonders on the

81

bladder); gentian (for both aperitifs and worms); the *lot*.

— And Evelyn—Mr Herbison—helps you in all this?

— He did, until he joined the Great Herbalist in the Skies; it was another unfortunate labelling mix-up. We were having a herb-tasting and what he thought was a compote of sorrel and coriander was in fact deadly nightshade and henbane. It was very sad, but, well, you know ... there's always heartsease.

— Thank you, Ms Herbison.

— Thank *you*. We're switched off, are we? What about nipping over to the local? It's only four miles and it's Wednesday; they do a very good steak-and-kidney on Wednesday. Good, plain, old-fashioned cooking; no fancy trimmings. Old Ma Gregson, the landlady, wouldn't know her fennel from her ribwort. Thank God they're not all like her; we'd be out of business. Come on: I'm dying for a Guinness; get rid of the taste of that goddam hyssop.

Mad fools of gardeners go out in the pouring
      rain
To prove they're Anglo-Saxon
They rarely put their macks on;
Each puts on rubber boots and squelches through
      moist terrain,
Then leaves the mud and silt on
The Wilton.
In high-rise flats when it's pouring cats and dogs
      they stay indoors
But the moment it teems each gardener seems to
      find essential chores;
They stayed in the Ark on Noah's remark
                  "It's pissing down again!..."
But mad fools of gardeners go out in the pouring
      rain.

A gardener's wife
Spends much of her life
Distraught
Because her old man seems to act
As though he's very slightly cracked.
Her efforts to drum
In common sense come
To naught
For as he rules o'er his dominion
Any feminine opinion
Isn't sought.
When informed by the met that the outlook's wet
          she wouldn't care two hoots
If he'd just take off his filthy dirty boots...

Mad fools of gardeners go out in the pouring
    rain.
They do it just for show-off
Or thinking it will go off.
They get more delight than a Spaniard might
       on a rain-swept Spanish plain;
Their wellies, if they're lucky,
All yukky.
They will watch the box through an equinox;
       at the slightest hint of floods
When it rains stair-rods these awkward sods
       go out to dig some spuds.
When it really pelts even hard-boiled Celts
       in their butts and bens remain—
But mad fools of gardeners
      get rather boring
        ruining the flooring
          having been out in the
           pouring
            rain.

House Plants

WE HAVE QUATERMASS trouble. I know the serial has been off the air for years—but we still sit with our armchairs pushed hard back against the wall at the far end of the room, wondering when the Thing is going to get us. Let me explain.

Some five years ago the lady of the house was given a stunted little plant in a very nasty cheap china pot, obviously bought in a charitable mood at a jumble. The plant had a few straggly bits of thin, needle-like foliage; one's first impulse was to dump it in the dustbin. The lady of the house said no, Mrs Pritchard (the donor) was a dear, well-meaning woman who did valiant work for Age Concern (hinting that any minute now I would be in need of her services) and if ever she came to tea, which God forbid, the first thing she would want to know was where we'd put her perishing plant. So, grudingly, it was allowed to stay. It was re-potted, in a pot *not* marked "A Present from Whitley Bay", and placed on a shelf at the shallow end of the front parlour.

The plant was identified with no great certainty as one of the asparagus ferns; if you want to be fussy, either *A myersii* or *A plumosus*. The uncertainty deepened when we looked up both of them in Holy Writ, and found *A myersii* described as "neat, compact, height 1/2ft, spread 12 in" and *A plumosus* as "compressed in shape, height 12 in, requires little or no trimming". Because Mrs Pritchard's donation hadn't been on the shelf a week before it decided to take over. New shoots appeared, usually two at a time and heading in different directions; fronds and tentacles reached along the shelf, over lampshades and up, along, and down the other side of pictures on the wall; ashtrays and other *objets d'art* had to be moved out of its way—not that we need have bothered, because in its relentless progress it would have brushed them aside or gone round, over, or under them.

It was when it started to embrace a small framed photograph of my mother at the other end of the shelf that we decided it could have nothing to do with the asparagus family, and began calling it Quatermass. The more it was re-potted, the greater its wanderlust. Encouraged, admittedly, by the lady of the house saying, "And when are we going to see some new babies, then?" and singing "Spread A Little Happiness" to it first thing in the morning.

It now dominates the room, and it knows it. Any female visitor of a nervous disposition sitting within range and feeling it first tickling the back of her neck and then advancing stealthily in the direction of her cleavage rises suddenly and says she's just remembered she parked her car on a resident's parking space and she'd better dash in case of warden trouble. We now live mostly in the kitchen, leaving the front room to the sitting tenant. The day it gets a hold on the banisters and starts coming upstairs, we're selling; not Quatermass (there would be difficulty in finding a buyer), but the house.

This is the trouble with house plants; they can make a room—they can make it very attractive indeed, especially on a grey dreary day in November—but they make it their way and no-one else's. And they can be expensive. The attractive little kangaroo vine (*Cissus antartica*, though what a kangaroo was doing anywhere down near the Falklands, Heaven alone knows) which you put on the rather wobbly occasional table over there in the corner, grows in that bounding way kangaroos have to a height of five or six feet, and the table looks silly. The logical move would be to get rid of the kangaroo and buy an African violet. You don't; you buy a larger, firmer, and much dearer table.

The neat little hedera dangling from the middle shelf of the china cupboard thrives and prospers until the danglings are down on the carpet and in danger of getting caught up in the Hoover. It would be sensible to get at it with the secateurs, but it looks so attractive you move it up to the top shelf and stow away the bits of china which were up there in the cupboard under the stairs. And then have to get the steps out to reach up and water it.

In the fulness of time, the maidenhair fern in attractive mock-Wedgwood container suspended by hook and chain high up on the wall behind the telly leaves a nasty mark on the wall. If commonsense prevailed, you'd take it down and give it in revenge to Mrs Pritchard, but no: much better give the whole room a fresh coat of emulsion in that nice magnolia

shade if we can just remember what it looked like, and then re-hang the maidenhair fern because it looks just right there high up in that corner. It is the plants who lay down both the law and the lay-out of a room; the householders fit in accordingly, moving the sofa from where it's been for years because the philodendron will get more light on that side.

Considering they get free board and lodging and the best of care and attention, some house plants are extraordinarily fussy. Several boarders sharing the same room make you appreciate how the ward sister in a busy hospital must feel with each patient having his or her own individual list of complaints, requests and demands. Elderly inmates like the aspidistra and the rubber plant need sponging down regularly; the begonia doesn't like direct sun and keeps asking for the curtains to be drawn, which causes trouble with the pelargonium who objects to being in the shade. The monstera (the one with the leaves which look as though they've been shredded) complains if it's in a draught; the cyclamen turns queasy if anyone lights a coal fire; when the azalea wants a drink of water, which is pretty often, woe betide whoever's on duty if there is a suspicion of lime in it. There's a thing called the dieffenbachia which is just about the most awkward in-patient ever; it can't stand draughts, it has a relapse if the room temperature goes either up or down, it's allergic to fumes even when a cigarette-lighter is lit in the next room, and it never stops asking for another glass of water. Luckily it is also highly poisonous and rarely asked in.

Credit, though, where credit is due. All the time television has been doing its damnedest to kill the art of conversation stone dead, house plants have been doing their little bit to preserve it. Intelligent adults who would never think of exchanging a word en passant with the buddleia in their garden, wax eloquent on the most intimate subjects to their house plants.

Chez nous, the conversation—admittedly one-sided—is oblique, direct contact having had no effect apart from perhaps a grunt from behind the evening paper. The calceolaria, say, is chosen as the confidante ... some people are in a grumpy mood tonight, aren't they, just because there was another signals failure at Clapham and their train was half an hour late, but never mind, my precious, you'll always have me to give you your drinkies. Or the coleus is put wise to the existing financial situation ... don't you worry, dear, old Scroogums may not get it into his head that because inflation's gone down 0.3 per cent in the last month it doesn't mean that Double Gloucester hasn't gone up 4p the quarter in the supermarket, but *you* understand, don't you, my poppet?

If the lady of the house is overheard saying in the bathroom " ... there, now, that's freshened up both of us, hasn't it, all that lovely steam, and we'll give you a nice dab with the suds from the Badedas because we want you looking your best when mother comes for the weekend", she is not necessarily speaking to someone sharing her bath-water. Or even to the loofah. She's talking to the rubber plant. It's extraordinary: you can't imagine anyone rabbitting on like that to the radishes or the spring onions out in the back garden. Not with the neighbours listening.

But indoors there is nothing like a good heart-to-heart chat with the cineraria.

Few of us, with Double Gloucester up 4p the quarter, can afford a conservatory which of course is the answer; if you're going to share your living quarters with house plants, try to make sure they're ones you'll get on with. The great thing is not to overdo it. I have, or had, some fairly well-britched friends who owned the penthouse flat on top of one of those modern blocks with worrying silent lifts. Their main room was so filled with exotic, semi-tropical plants that you felt you were nowhere near Bognor, but in the depth of the Brazilian jungle. Dense foliage had to be brushed aside before you could sit down; having brushed it aside, it either swished back in your face or tendrils got under your armpits. Because of the rare orchids, guests and things like After Eights melted in the heat like Mrs Thatcher's smile when asked an awkward one by Mr Powell. The Tarzan effect was added to by a number of macaws and a toucan or two perched on the branches of paw-paws, or finding things in your hair; if you managed to see a corner free of undergrowth and sat down on the sofa, you had an uneasy feeling that there might be a boa-constrictor under it. This is really going too far; the odd thing is that the owners, while groping for yet another tissue to mop the perspiration or wipe a lizard off the pouffe, kept saying, "If you can't have a proper garden and get out in the fresh air, this is the next best thing."

Kept in their place and not allowed to gain the upper hand, house plants can be an asset to any room. They should be treated as you would treat all other house guests: welcomed, made to feel at home, looked after, given a drink at the right time, and if they interfere with routine got rid of as quickly as possible and not invited back.

For some eight years now there has been an ashtray—*the* ashtray, the one that matters— positioned approximately fifteen inches to the right of my favourite armchair. The other evening I reached out and found myself flicking ash into a primula obconica which had been moved because it caught the light there and looked so pretty on that little table. The ashtray was at the other end of the room, hidden behind the hippeastrum. This is the sort of thing— when house plants are given preference over the guy who pays the rates—which has got to be nipped in the bud, if not lower down. Chesterton wrote:

> On the wrong side of the door
> The green plant groweth, menacing...

I know just how he felt. He had Quatermass trouble, I'll bet.

I talk to my plants.
I always say "Good-morning" to my cactus
And "Night-night, Busy Lizzie—time for bed."
Others use Baby Bio, which can act as
A stimulant. I chat 'em up instead.
I read my begonias Betjeman's rhymes
Or bits of obits which appear in *The Times*;
When my cyclamen's sickly, it perks up no end
To be told who's Antonia Fraser's new friend;
And my primula burgeons in various hues
When I give it the gist of the Nine O'clock News.
But one night last week I was rudely rebuffed:
My plants answered back, saying loudly "Get
    stuffed!"
"Stop yakkity-yakking!" they cried in a chorus
And an African violet added "You *bore* us!"
My coleus threatened to call the police
If I didn't turn Trappist and leave it in peace;
"For God's sake, belt up!" said the ferns in my
    flat,
"Just pass round the drink, dear, and less bloody
    chat."
So now when I water, not one word is said.
I give them their Bio, and cut them stone dead.

Showing Off

"*COMPETITIVE?*" SAID MRS Hopson of Henfield. She used the word as though she had been bitten by a tsetse fly. "Oh, no. No, no, never. We just do it for our own pleasure and, we hope, other people's."

"It" was the embellishment—the transformation, in fact—of a none-too-stately home in Sussex by the most breathtaking display of flower arrangements . . . at the entrance, in the hall, in all the main rooms, even in the master bathroom where if the owners had known that their bidet was going to be rendered impractical by a falling cascade of roses, gladioli, lilies and carnations, they would have removed their toothbrushes which seemed to me to need retufting. Admission 50p, including homemade tea, all proceeds to the British Legion. And I had just decided that by and large gardeners are a selfish lot, ready to show off the delights of their gardens to an impressionable few, none too keen on sharing them with the common herd.

I was really thinking of myself, but it seemed fairer to embrace the whole gardening fraternity and dismiss the idea that it was only I who shied back like a nervous deer when the Vicar suggested Throwing

The Garden Open in aid of the Roof Restoration Fund. I mean, imagine. All those people galumphing all over the place, flattening the alyssum and the aubrietia along the edge of that border, pot-holing the grass with their stilettos, and being overheard on their way out saying, well, I must say, I didn't think much of his roses, the ones Aunt Lil had at her cremation would have knocked the black spots off his any day. And when it was all over, the roof still leaking immediately above one's own pew. Stately homes and Beverley Nichols, I know, get Thrown Open year after year. Medals have been struck for lesser acts of self-sacrifice and service to the community.

I had just reached the sweeping conclusion that most of us are not only the do-it-yourself but also the keep-it-to-yourself type of gardener when along came Mrs Hopson, and there must be hundreds like her. Mrs Hopson, when she's not ripping off the leading roles for the Henfield Amateur Operatic Society, is the genius presiding over the Henfield Flower Club, affiliated to the National Association of Flower Arrangement Societies of Great Britain (NAFAS). The Flower Club, membership seventy-plus and a waiting-list, meets once a month for lectures by alleged experts on conditioning, ie, bashing the ends of stems before putting them in vases. What the members really enjoy, though, is the chance of descending on some large house in the district and smothering it in floral arrangements. They also make very good sponge cakes. All they get out of it is enjoyment; no cups, no trophies, not even a certificate for the best arranged floral bidet. The competitive side of things they left to the men, said Mrs Hopson.

How commendable; how true. In the North of England, where I was born, more blood was spilt through Annual Horticultural Shows than through unemployment, the closing of pits, or Philip Snowdon. In mining communities like Ashington the male pursuits of the menfolk, when not down the pits, were leeks, sex and whippets. In that order. Whole shows were devoted to leeks; outsiders like artichokes and gatecrashers like celeriac weren't allowed to enter. Battle stations were drawn in the cause of leeks and nothing else.

For weeks before the actual outbreak of hostilities, the utmost vigilance had to be observed by gardeners and allotment-holders training their leeks to be in the peak of condition just in time for the great day. Traps were set against saboteurs or leek-jackers; desperate men sat up all night guarding their leeks with loaded shotguns and sniffer dogs. There were filthy accusations and counter-accusations of on the one hand leek-breeders injecting hormones into recalcitrant leeks, even blowing them up with bicycle pumps or having them transferred for large sums of money like footballers, and from the other side of leeks being doped with sedatives or chlorophyll just when they were ready for the ring. In a way, it was a sort of gradually diminishing hereditary process; in earlier days up in those parts cattle-rustling was the "in" thing. My own ancestors, by the evidence available, were pretty good at it; quite a few of them were hanged for it; the family is rather proud of the fact. Later, when the North became namby-pamby, it was woman-rustling and then salmon poaching; now—though these two activities still flourish—with the advance of civilisation into the twentieth century, it's leeks.

Marrows are the only other vegetable to come anywhere near them in underground activity and SAS technique. Just when they're the equivalent of nine months gone and certain of at least an Honorary Mention in their class, they get nicked off by the stem and appear in jars of homemade marrow preserve at WI fêtes across the border on the other side of the Tweed. This is regarded as legitimate and good clean fun; but fouling up a leek's chances on the eve of the Annual Show brings out the Hotspur in all true Northumbrians, and the repercussions can be dire. Hell, up in those parts, hath no fury like that of a potential leek champion done out of his rosette, certificate, or cup.

The NAFAS ladies would never behave like that. If one of their flower arrangements were mugged or nobbled just before the off they would, I feel sure, smile sadly, blame it on too much violence being shown on television and arrange another one in record time, even if it meant snatching the last digitalis out of the President's herbaceous border. About the Henfield chaps, I'm not so sure. Some at least of the combatant spirit of the North seems to have seeped down South, especially round the dates of Annual Shows. This is the age of investigative journalism, informers, grasses, and—spelt the other way—leaks. There has been leaked to me a confidential copy of the Hon Secretary's report of the Fletchley Horticultural Society's last Annual Show. It

seems to suggest that, while the Society's members may not actually appear in Court on charges of assault and grievous bodily harm as often as horticulturists up North, a certain amount of skullduggery goes on . . .

ANNUAL SHOW

Despite torrential rain which on several occasions forced the judges to seek shelter in the refreshment tent, the Society's 57th Annual Show attracted a record entry and proved an unqualified success. As usual, the event was held in the grounds of "Greenfingers", Thatcher's Way, Lower Fletchley, by kind permission of the Society's President, Alderman Arthur Plenderleith, JP, and Mrs Plenderleith. After a few well-chosen opening remarks by the Chairman of the Show Committee, Mr James Plenderleith, Mrs Arthur Plenderleith was presented with a bouquet of lunaria, tuberoses, and St John's wort by little Samantha Plenderleith, 6, niece of our indefatigable Hon Secretary, Mr Frank Plenderleith.

During the afternoon teas were provided by the Ladies' Committee under the supervision of the Chairman's good lady, Mrs James Plenderleith; and a popular innovation this year was the refreshment marquee, more than adequately stocked and expertly managed by Plenderleith's Off-Licence in Chapel Street. Our thanks are due to this old-established family business for supplying everything on their special guaranteed sale or return terms, though happily on this occasion no such proviso proved necessary. There had been some doubt about the Society being granted a license for this additional feature of the Show, but objections both from the Methodists and various licensed victuallers in the district were soon routed. We were no doubt fortunate in the fact that Alderman Plenderleith was on the Bench when our application was heard!

The task of the judges—Alderman and Mrs Plenderleith, the Chairman, Hon Secretary, and Hon Treasurer (Mr Herbert Plenderleith) and acting as a co-opted member, Mrs Eccles (Alderman Plenderleith's sister-in-law, and always a welcome visitor to "Greenfingers" and to Fletchley)—cannot have been easy, as the exhibits were without exception of a remarkably high standard. The main awards were as follows:

The *Arthur Plenderleith Bowl* for the Best Exhibit in the Show, presented by the President in memory of his late father, Capt Bertram ("Beetroot") Plenderleith of REME, was won for the seventh successive year by Mr Thomas Plenderleith of Coltsfoot Cottages. A record, surely, in the art of gaining major horticultural awards, certainly in the Fletchley and Lower Fletchley area! As in previous years and to save expense, the winner again kindly agreed to have the two dots signifying "ditto" engraved on the trophy rather than his full name; he had, in fact, already arranged for this symbol to be put on the bowl for the years up to and including 1990, when he intends to stop exhibiting himself and—as he puts it—give some up-and-coming youngster (Tom junior, perhaps, who knows?) a chance. Well done yet again, Tom senior!

The *Lucy Plenderleith Cup* for the Best Collection of Six Onions (the "Onion Oscar") caused one of the few minor contretemps of the afternoon. This was one of the last classes to be judged, and when the panel reemerged from the refreshment tent it was announced to everyone's surprise that the winning exhibit was No 18 (Mr Josh Manderson of Clapper's Lane Farm), with Mrs Herbert Plenderleith, wife of our hard-working Hon Treasurer, as runner-up. The Hon Treasurer very rightly pointed out that Clapper's Lane Farm was at least a quarter-of-a-mile outside the Fletchley Rural District Council area and that by the rules of the Society Mr Manderson was ineligible to compete. It was found, in any case, that the real winning exhibit was No 13 (Mrs Plenderleith's onions), the confusion having been caused by liquid of some kind being spilt over the judges' programme and causing the number to be smudged. Josh, to his credit, took the setback in good part and no-one was more concerned than he when he reversed his car into the Hon Treasurer's new Metro on his way out.

The *Amy Plenderleith Marrow Medallion* was awarded to Mrs Armstrong, who it will be remembered was married just over eight months ago in St Luke's to Mr Jack Armstrong and who is of course the younger daughter of Mr and Mrs

Charles Plenderleith. Owing to circumstances beyond her control, Mrs Armstrong was unable to be among those present and the award was accepted on her behalf by Dr Chapman, who was on his way to see her in any case and said it was just what was wanted to take her mind off things. The winning marrow weighed 9 lbs 7 oz, measured 4' 11" from stem to stern, and had a circumference of no less than 41" (1.487 metres) at its widest part. Dr Chapman said he would place it carefully at Mrs Armstrong's side, and no end of amusement was caused in the refreshment tent by Mrs Eccles—who, coming as she does from Kingston-on-Thames, has a keenly developed sense of humour—saying she hoped the doctor wouldn't get the two of them mixed up when the time came.

Other awards included:
Best Parsnips — Mr Thomas Plenderleith
Best in Cauliflower and Cabbage Class — Mr Thomas Plenderleith
Best Display of Leeks (6) — Mr Thomas Plenderleith
Curliest Kale in the Show — Mr Thomas Plenderleith
Best Herb Collection — The Vicar*
Frank Plenderleith Trophy for Best Perpetual Spinach — Mrs Frank Plenderleith
Best Exhibit by Child Under 15 — Miss Samantha Plenderleith
Comedy Class: Most Provocative Shaped Cucumber — Mrs Eccles
Best Outdoor Tomatoes — Mrs Taylor,

Waggon and Horses Inn*

Best Indoor Tomatoes — Mrs Taylor, Waggon and Horses Inn*

Best Maincrop Potatoes — Mr Thomas Plenderleith

Best Maincrop Runners — Mr Thomas Plenderleith

Best Maincrop Peas ("Alderman") — Alderman Plenderleith, JP

*These awards, though not gained strictly on merit, were deemed by the judges to be politic, the Vicar having given the Society free use of the Church Hall for winter meetings in return for Harvest Festival decorations, and Mrs Taylor having always been so nice about hours.

The first prize in the raffle (bottle of vintage Californian Pouilly kindly donated by Plenderleith's Off-Licence) was won by Mrs Frank Plenderleith, wife of our ever-conscientious Hon Sec. There was considerable amusement and not a little good-natured ribbing when the winner's name was announced! However, Mrs Plenderleith sportingly handed back the prize to be re-raffled, and by a happy coincidence it was won on the second time round by her cousin, Mr Basil Plenderleith. Thereby "keeping it in the family", as the President wittily remarked.

The balance and loss account, apart from the healthy profit from the refreshment tent which of course does not accrue to the Society, shows a deficit of £87.00, but several bills are yet to come to hand and until the Hon Treasurer gets back from holiday in Majorca the Society's present financial position cannot be accurately ascertained.

(signed)
James Plenderleith, Chairman, Show Committee
Frank Plenderleith, Hon Secretary

Well, that, I suppose, is show business. But it seems to me that we males could learn a lot from the selfless, altruistic approach of the ladies who show off the delights of their gardens with no thought of glory or personal gain. Not that the Vicar need have any more ideas about me being Thrown Open just because a few more slates have been blown off his roof. Beverley Nichols may fall for it, and all credit to him; not this guy. For one thing, it would mean tidying up the toolshed. I'm not having that thrown open to the public and the public seeing all those empties.

D an Cupid had a garden
As everybody knows
In which he grew (this, too, you knew)
The perfect English rose.
But Dan's purse-strings were slender things
Drawn tight as Cupid's bows;
A fact made clear as, year by year,
The price of roses rose.

Dan Cupid changed his garden
To cabbage, spuds, and kale.
D Cupid wasn't stupid:
He offered them for sale
And all he grows he shows at shows
And wins enormous prizes.
He'll do it again next autumn, when
The price of roses rises.

Coming to Terms Again

We got halfway through the alphabet—as far as K for Kitchen Gardening—before nipping indoors for that much-needed drink. In practice this happens much earlier, usually after B for Bending or C for Clearing Up, and certainly long before D for Digging. There is still, however, a great deal to be done . . .

Lawn, Mowing of Some considerable time before we went over to decimal coinage, I was bribed with the sum of threepence, in addition to what was known as my Saturday penny, for mowing the front lawn. I had difficulty in getting the money out of my father, who usually said he'd no change on him less than a sixpence and had obviously no intention of doubling up. The lawn-mower weighed a ton, or seemed to; it had one of those metal baskets loosely attached to it to catch the clippings. If you mowed at all *allegro* or *vivace*, the clippings shot over the top of the basket or splayed out past each side of it; when, in spite of this, the container was full of clippings, it fell off and the clippings landed back where they'd started on the lawn and had to be swept up. The model was called, I remember, the Lightweight Easi-Mow, rather like calling Orson Welles svelte.

Now I have no lawn, which is sad but at least does away with wormcasts, moles, fairy rings and moss. But I watch with envy the modern school of motorised mowists gliding effortlessly over their green swards in souped-up, three-speed geared, power-assisted steering models, some even lolling back on the pillion seat waving to less fortunate pushers and shovers. When you mow your lawn, you should have in mind those immaculately parallel stripes in contrasting shades of green seen at, say, Lords or Wembley before Ian Botham or Glenn Hoddle mess them up. If your stripes are not absolutely parallel but have that unfortunate wobble halfway up or down them, the lady of the house assumes that you've had a couple before going a-mowing, adding that one of these fine days you'll be breathalysed and found over the limit and charged with being drunk and disorderly while driving a lawn-mower, and very pretty that's going to look in the evening paper.

Apart from mowing, all a lawn requires is rolling, brushing, raking, aerating, watering, spiking for drainage and root growth, weeding, fertilising, feeding, top dressing, and scarifying. After that, the rest is easy; all you have to do is trim the edges and then start the whole procedure all over again. Scarifying, yes; this means taking your lawn rake, or someone else's lawn rake if you haven't one of your own, and raking the living bejesus out of the lawn in late autumn. It is known to the experts as scarifying, and don't ask me why; perhaps to frighten the wits out of any worm contemplating casting.

The only faintly plausible excuse for getting out of

mowing the lawn is to say that the grass is too wet; difficult during a prolonged drought. The easy way is to dig up the damn thing and put down crazy paving; but this is mean, deceitful, and in a way sad. When I did it, I felt rotten for hours. Oddly enough I miss it, wormcasts, moss, and all.

Manuring With the increasing popularity of the horseless carriage, this has become more and more difficult to do in anything like a natural sort of way. Few of us have the opportunity, let alone the nerve, to follow Her Majesty's Household Cavalry along the Mall on some State occasion with a bucket and shovel in the hope. And—here I may have been unfortunate—the signs in country lanes saying FARMYARD MANURE £1 THE BAG prove misleading: seven-eighths straw to one-eighth what you're after. I get the feeling that the livestock on the farms I've patronised lately must be on that F-for-fibre diet, and none too regular in their motions.

The thing is, of course, to have your own compost heap, adding to it contributions from the kitchen like gone-off outside lettuce leaves and potato peelings, but *not* left-over spaghetti bolognaise or the heels of Spotted Dicks. There are three things which are God's gifts to the four-star compost heap:

(1) Spent hops. If you live near a brewery, they might let you have some. Anyway, they're bound to show you round and offer you a sample of the product at the end of the tour.

(2) Sewage sludge and rape. With names like those, the compost heap is the only place for them.

(3) Wool shoddy. This lets off nitrogen ad nauseam

and is a must for compost heaps. Look up the Yellow Pages and get in touch with your nearest wool shoddy retailer.

The trouble with compost heaps is that, like mattresses, they need turning over at regular intervals, and they look awful. Which is why, as was made clear earlier, there are no fairies at the bottom of my garden. The whole manure syndrome has become fraught; but you could buy a camel. I am told they are the most generous and accommodating animals in supplying gardeners' requirements, and that their end product has a remarkable effect on dahlias.

Nurseries, dealing with Nurseries are so called because the male nurses on the staff have been trained, rightly, to treat all customers as children. Rather naughty children, with kindergarden ideas about wanting their petunias bedded out before the risk of late frost is over by perhaps the middle of June, and inclined to be petulant when they can't have the fuchsia which has been set aside for some other spoilt brat.

Never argue with the nurses in nurseries; they know what is good for you, and any ideas you may have which don't fit in with their own will be dismissed as heresy, new-fangled, or well, we wouldn't advise it, but if that's the way you want it don't say we didn't warn you! Whatever you say, you will leave the operating theatre without the cotoneaster you were after ("transplant it at this time o' the year, asking for trouble, that is") and with the box of asters they made up their mind to sell you as soon as they saw you opening the boot of the car.

Over-watering Avoid in cases, and even single bottles, of whisky, gin, vodka, etc, and in almost all greenhouse and indoor plants. Careful, though: what the lady of the house calls Dolly Brolly, the umbrella plant, has a thirst which not even Alcoholics Anonymous can do much about, whereas most cacti can get through the winter without touching a drop of the stuff. In our greenhouse, where the cacti are neatly arranged all round Dolly Brolly, this makes watering tricky; one badly-aimed splurt from the can ruins the total abstainers' reputation and leaves the lush complaining about room service.

Pruning As long as you follow the rules about pruning roses, there should be no difficulty. There are two: (1) prune hard back in November, and only lightly early in the following year; and (2) prune back only lightly in November, and then hard back early in the following year.

You should either prune just above an outward-facing bud or shoot, or just below it and and above the next one down. Make the cut diagonally, some experts advising sloping outwards and others inward towards the centre of the bush. In certain cases you should prune back to two or three shoots from the junction with the main stem; in other cases, rather more; and in still other cases, slightly less. Never prune too close to the growth bud in case of damaging it; on the other hand, if you prune too far away from the growth bud you get what are known as snags, which means you've damaged not the bud itself but the stem on which the bud was thinking of budding. Weak growths should be pruned back harder than vigorous ones; at the same time, very vigorous growths should be pruned back even harder than the weaklings. Just stick to these hard-and-fast rules and you'll have no trouble at all except perhaps a few snags.

Question-Time, Gardeners' If you're ever asked to take Bill Sowerbutts' place on this one, here is a tip worth remembering. I learned it years ago when for a spell I was chairman of the BBC's *Brains Trust*—long before your time: Huxley, Joad, Commander Campbell, and that twinkling little genius, Dr Bronowski. When he didn't wish to become involved in a question, Bruno would give me an off-camera signal indicating "include me out". He would then wait while the other three waffled and floundered long enough to get beyond hailing distance of the subject matter, give another off-screen signal making it clear that he was now ready to participate, and say, "Of course, what the questioner *weally* asked was . . ." It's a sure-fire way of endearing yourself to the audience and putting the rest of the panel in their place.

Once, at a special edition of *Gardener's Question Time*, I was among the plants. I mean, among the questioners planted in the audience. I wanted to know why my *Sparmannia africana* had given up flowering when otherwise it looked as fit as a fiddle. Perhaps I phrased it badly; I said I was in the habit of cultivating a good deal of hemp at home. For weeks after, the neighbours gave me some very strange looks. The four experts went on and on about sparmannia, but none of them really knew the answer.

Nor did they to the question put by Frank Muir,

who was another of the plants. He'd got rid of some cypress trees in order to lay down a hard tennis court in his garden and healthy young cypresses were coming up along both baselines, which makes serving difficult even for John McEnroe. What Mr Muir wanted to know was should he get rid of the cypresses or take up the tennis court and also perhaps take up clock golf? He got precious little change out of that one, either, though Professor Alan Gemmell went on at considerable length about *Cupressocyparis leylandii* hating lime. Mr Muir was heard muttering that when he played tennis he only drank an occasional sip of the stuff when changing ends and mopping down.

Re-potting   As with some unfortunate humans, many plants become pot-bound; they need lebensraum, like fast-breeding council tenants. Hold the pot-bound plant firmly in the left hand and tap the bottom of the inverted pot gently with a trowel held in your right hand. If left-handed, do it the other way round; it will make no difference, because absolutely nothing will happen. Continue to tap and then bash until the bound pot smashes into smithereens and the bound earth round the bound plant disintegrates and lands in the gardener's crutch or crotch. Place bits of the broken pot at the bottom of another pot to act as crocks for drainage; this is known as the rotation of pots or, down on the South coast where I live, the old crocks' race.

Before re-potting, the new pots—and indeed all pots—should be thoroughly hosed out, rinsed, scrubbed, disinfected with Jeyes' fluid, stood upside-down to dry out, and then carefully dusted to get rid

of germs, bacteria, aphids' fingerprints, etc. This is *absolutely essential*; it is also rarely if ever done except in high-class nurseries and gardening manuals.

Suckers Suckers are additive irritants like the service charge and VAT on restaurant bills. It is a widely-held belief that you recognise a sucker by it having seven leaflets instead of the usual five on each leaf; as there is no truth at all in this widely-held belief, do not waste valuable time counting your leaflets. Suckers should never be cut out in the way people are cut out of wills; they should be pulled off, like waders, and then rubbed out like typing errors, as when "years of maturing" comes out as "fears of manuring".

The real suckers, though, are ourselves: gardeners. The people who assemble the annual gardening catalogues know they have only to superimpose little notices saying NEW! or NOVELTY!! or SENSATION: ORDER NOW, SUPPLIES LIMITED!!! for us to reach out for the Biro and fill in the order form. There's a regular advertisement for a fast-growing hedge (faster even than *Lawsoniana*) covered in masses of Guaranteed All-the-Year-Round Spectacular Blossom, with a nauseatingly happy young couple beaming up at it and collecting armfuls of guaranteed spectacular blossom . . . the suckers fall for that one every time.

And those miniature peach trees, your own superb peaches in profusion THIS YEAR, can be grown on your patio or loggia, even your kitchen window-sill, complete with elegant Grecian-style container, full instructions included, ONLY £4.99 plus £2.85 part p and p, money returned in full if not completely satisfied, ORDER NOW while stocks last. I fell for that one myself eight years ago; last summer, whenever I went near it, the lady of the house said she'd ordered in some more ice cream and if the guaranteed profusion of luscious fruit was ripe enough was there any chance of having one *pêche Melba* divided between the two of us?

"Fast-growing" seems to be the operative word which attracts suckers; some enterprising horticulturist ought to go up north to my homeland on the banks of the Tweed, where they are having trouble with something called *Heracleum mantegazzianum*, or hogweed to you. In April it's about six inches high; by July it's well over fifteen feet and just beginning to spread itself. A harassed spokesman for the Borders Regional Council said, when pressed, "You can *hear* it grow." Now *that*, put on the market, would make a bomb with the suckers: what they're after is instant results. Not even the fact that it causes skin rash, acute blistering, recurrent dermatitis, and the news that the Edinburgh hospitals are filling up nicely with people who've brushed against it, would put them off. Suckers, myself included, rarely read the small print.

Taking Cuttings Do so, whenever offered. If next-door says "You know that pelargonium you admired—the one with the sort of variegated leaf—I've taken some cuttings of it and every one I've taken has taken: you wouldn't like one or two, would you?" take them. At once.

Under-watering (see *Over-watering*, but leave hose unconnected to tap.) This is an aspect of the gardener's life which gives rise to brittle, sophisticated dialogue on the lines of:

— The garden's looking terribly dry.
— M'm.
— Those roses in the top bed look absolutely parched, poor things.
— M'm.
— And the forecast says continuing warm and sunny in the South; occasional showers, some heavy and prolonged, in Scotland.
— M'm.
— Next-door was out hosing the minute he got back from London, and you know what torture commuting's like these days. I wonder the poor soul's not worn out.
— M'm.
— Isn't it funny? Some people, even after a hard day's grind, seem to find the energy to do what's got to be done in the garden. Other people are just bone idle.
— M'm.
— Mrs Palmer in "Teesmaid" (you know she comes from Stockton?) says they're thinking of getting one of those rotating spray things you see on lawns in Beverly Hills that you just switch on and leave it. Of course Mr Palmer's an area manager for Lombards and I've no doubt can afford . . . Where are you going?
— I am going to hose the garden. Not because I wish to do so; not because I have any faith in the weather forecast proving accurate; but solely because the gentle pitter-patter of the hose-water falling on the leaves of the roses out there will make a highly desirable change from the non-

stop nagging indoors.

> *Exit. Pause until slam of back door.*

— It never fails. It may take a little time, but it never fails.

Vine Cultivation Until comparatively recently, this was largely confined to districts in France like the Loire, the champagne departments, and the Rhone valley; and to bits of Germany with ridiculous names like Niederlederhosenrudesheimwinkelsee. In the last few years the cultivation of the grape in the United Kingdom has increased enormously; in pubs where not so long ago you'd have been considered sissy if you asked for a small glass of dry white, barmaids don't even bat their mascara.

The great thing about vine cultivation is to select the vine, the vineyard, and the vintage which suits you and then cultivate both them and your wine merchant so that he can always let you have a case at short notice when other cultivators land on you unexpectedly for the weekend. Cultivate them like mad. Don't hurry in your selection of the many types of vines available; take your time, do it leisurely, try out as wide a selection as possible (there are many travelling salesmen only too ready to arrange little tasting sessions without obligation to purchase). Once you have decided on, say, the Nuits-St-Georges '79 or even the Côte de Beaune '80, cultivate it assiduously and with loving care, never cutting back or pruning unless forced to do so on medical advice.

And remember that we in this country are still comparative novices in vine cultivation. If we are to take our place alongside our more experienced colleagues in the bistros of the Common Market, we have a lot of catching up to do. *Santé. A la vôtre.* Cheers.

Weeding   It can be fun, you know. Imagine that you're opening for England against Australia at Lords, and that every weed you pull up counts towards a brilliant century, scored in record time and gaining you the Man of the Match award: chickweed a single, groundsel a smartly-run two, four for a nettle, and a really tough plantain a clean six into the Tavern. Or that you're doing battle with HM Inspector of Taxes, and that for every hundred weeds claimed you get a rebate of, say, fifty pounds on your annual assessment. Or that each weed represents someone you can't stand the sight of on television: out with Terry Wogan, up with Esther Rantzen, and over your shoulder with that little horror in *The Waltons*.

Or suggest to the lady of the house that with a little more bending and stooping she might squeeze into a size 16 instead of an 18. The trouble here is that she usually pulls up the nigella seedlings and leaves the speedwell because it looks so attractive and has those pretty little blue flowers.

X   Apart from being the mark you made to stop the neighbours finding out you've won the pools, this is the symbol for cross-pollination and the expectancy of the patter of tiny little hybrid feet. For years people who won't leave well alone have been trying to cross a tomato with an artichoke and calling the result either a tomachoke or an artito; if they succeeded, it would go down in the official records as *Cyrana scolymus x lycopersicum esculutum*, and probably taste of parsnip. I wouldn't advise it. I toyed once with the idea of cross-breeding bearded irises, which are supposed to be the species most ready to put up with this sort of thing. I looked it up in Holy Writ, and the instructions began:

> Expose the stigma, wipe the pollen on its outer edge, cover with a waterproof bag and wait for the seed-pod to distend.

I gave up the idea at once; it's not the sort of thing you want discussed at coffee mornings. Leave it to the bees.

Y is for *Youth and Old Age* which, thank God, is the other name for

Zinnia: and without the two of them coming together, anyone compiling a glossary of gardening terms such as this would find that, like a dandelion's root, there is no end to it. Not that this list of gardeners' troubles is in any way complete. There has been no mention of layering or mulching, of cordoning or grafting, of heeling-in, pricking-out, dead-heading, or gumming. Or gnomes.

My heart, like Wordsworth's, always fills
With pleasure at the daffodils.
I wander lonely as a cloud
And think: this year they've done me proud.
These trumpeting King Alfreds ring
A fanfare to the right of Spring . . .
True harbingers of what's ahead—
A jocund Co, as Wordsworth said.

And three weeks later on, I wander
Lonely and cloud-like still, and ponder
On just how soon their blooms can fade,
Go brown round edges, half decayed,
And look—if we would but confess—
Really a rather horrid mess.
(Wordsworth by now, in well-turned phrases,
Was writing sonnets about daisies.)

One's gloom increases when one thinks
That daffodils (and phlox and pinks
And lupins and, let's face it, Man)
Enjoy their brief allotted span
And then, with no-one caring tuppence,
Receive their all too swift come-uppance.
(Wordsworth no doubt by now had done
Westminster Bridge, quiet as a nun.)

But just a minute. Think again.
In due course, even Wedgwood Benn,
His trumpet muted, will begin
To fade, and Nancy lose her grin
And Terry Wogan won't be here
And even VAT will disappear.
(Wordsworth, in this mood, would declare
That earth had naught to show more fair.)

The guy was right. What really matters
Are bulbs one plants and seeds one scatters.
And so my heart with pleasure fills
Thinking of next year's daffodils.

Gnomes

WELL, IT HAD to happen sooner or later. Goodness knows we've put it off for as long as possible. Writing a book with a title like "Gnomes and Gardens" and making only a fleeting reference to gnomes is like writing a biography of Abelard and just happening to mention at the foot of p 219 that around 1115, while a canon of Notre Dame, he met a girl called Heloise. And leaving it at that, without going into the trouble she got him into; not that the getting into trouble was all that one-sided.

Very well, then: gnomes. Let me re-state my personal point of view. I have absolutely nothing against gnomes. They are obviously harmless, inoffensive little creatures, bringing a great deal of happiness to a great many people, and with no unfortunate habits like mugging or showing holiday snaps or polluting the atmosphere by disseminating obnoxious fumes via either mechanical or human exhausts. As features of an English country garden, they neither require weeding nor do they attract green-fly. They seem enviably contented with life; they don't write letters to *The Times* about the Arts Council or the Government's economic strategy, if it possesses such a thing; they don't complain about BBC repeats or grizzle once a quarter when the gas bill comes in about it going up. Even a built-in, professional fault-finder like John Osborne would find it difficult to criticise them, except perhaps on aesthetic grounds. I just don't see their point, apart from the peaked one on top of those balaclava helmet things they seem to wear in all weathers.

I have some dear, good neighbours who—while remaining free of gnomes—have placed on one of the window-ledges at the front of their house a plaster-of-Paris cat (it may be china, or even papier mâché: whatever it is, it looks very realistic) crouched ready to pounce on a plaster-of-Paris-or-whatever mouse cringing on the next window-ledge. The cat has that look in its eyes which cats get just before saying "Gotcha"; the mouse is clearly paralysed by fear and unable to twitch a hair of its moustache. The pounce is obviously going to be difficult and even dangerous, involving taking off from window-ledge A and executing a sort of mid-air parabola before landing on window-ledge B for the kill.

Now that, I can see the point of. Between them, my neighbours' cat and mouse have given us more simple pleasure than all the Tom and Jerry cartoons put together, and without animation. In the gloaming, or if there's a slight sea mist and visibility is none too good, strangers passing in our midst suddenly stop in their tracks, clutch each other by the elbows and—thinking it's a real cat and a genuine mouse—point up to the window-ledges and stand spellbound, waiting for the law of the jungle to be enacted before their very eyes. As both cat and mouse have been on their respective ledges for eighteen years, naturally without moving a muscle, the spectators have a long wait ahead of them. Now there is point, or at least entertainment value when watched from behind your lace curtains, in that.

Passers-by seeing a gnome or coven of gnomes in a front garden react, if they react at all, in one of two ways ... "Look, Geoffrey, what a dear little gnome" or "Bloody gnomes all over the place, the woman must be potty." They then just carry on round the corner to the Chinese take-away, dismissing gnomes as irrelevant. Which, of course, they're not. They must mean *something*; they must fulfil some purpose; they must go on sitting year after year fishing on obviously dry land for some reason. I wish I knew what. It's a blank in one's admittedly limited mental equipment, like not being able to read shorthand or make head or tail of those chess problems in the Sunday papers.

Because you cannot dismiss gnomists as potty; I have another neighbour (I am surrounded by them) who is a charming, extremely intelligent individual, something high up in higher education, reads Sartre and has taught and lectured in Red China; the sort of person whom Mensa accepts without the qualifying test while the rest of us, doing our tables, have to think twice whether *mensa* is followed by *mensam* or there's another one in between. The first time she showed me round her garden, with what do I come face-to-face? The most enormous gnome, ruddy-complexioned, balaclava'd, jerkin-bound, beaming away like a sawn-off moron. "Er ... left here by the previous owners?" I said. "Oh, no," said Ms Mensa.

"I brought him with me. I'm very fond of him. His name's Kierkegaard."

How gnomes began, let alone why gardeners began fouling up their gardens with them, is vague. One has this nebulous notion that in some way, without quite knowing why, they're mixed up with leprechauns, the little people, the Brothers Grimm and Scandinavian wood-cutters, fertility symbols, and those seven dwarfs who stole all the scenes without much difficulty from that dreadful Snow White.

The fertility symbol theory, to which a lot of gnomers subscribe, seems especially dicey. For one thing, I don't know if you've noticed this, but all gnomes appear to be male. Naturally, a vast amount of research has been carried out before writing this chapter; not a gnome have I gnoted wearing high heels or carrying a handbag, not that carrying a handbag these days is any cast-iron criterion of gender. Yet there they all are, blissfully happy, grinning away, and not a dame in sight. It's the sort of subject best left to Katherine Whitehorn and the *Guardian's* Woman's Page, but it seems to me to strike the fertility argument fairly and squarely on its head.

There's an equally muzzy notion that in some way gnomes bring a garden good luck and ward off enemies and evil spirits and the like. Not much in that one, either, if you watch the cats picking their way delicately through a gnomery and doing their stuff on the polyanthus planted between them. And there's another school of thought, not yet comprehensive, which maintains that gnomes act as guardians of rich seams of precious metal and/or hidden treasure. If there's anything in that one, it would seem more sensible to get the spade out and start digging instead of leaving an obviously retarded midget to mark the spot. I suppose if a Gallup poll were conducted on why people have gnomes in their gardens, the results would be something like:

Well, I mean, they brighten the place up, don't they?	58%
I mean, like, y'know, they don't do any harm, do they?	29%
After all, it's a free country, innit?	4%
Don't Knows	9%

On all matters concerning gnomes I am among the 9 per cent. (Odd, isn't it; it's always 9 per cent who don't know. It's my belief that they do know but aren't saying, just to drive the psephologists mad adjusting their swingometers.) But my ignorance about gnomes (about gardens, too, you may say, which makes the writing of this book all the more strange) is abysmal. So abysmal that, conscientious as ever, I went to our excellent local reference library and asked a direct question of the Head Librarian, who blanches like celery whenever I appear, wondering what in God's name he's going to ask this time. "Have you anything," I said, "on gnomes?" Yes, indeed, said the Head Librarian, relieved, and after a few minutes' skirmishing in the rear premises returned with a massive tome which needed dusting down and clearly wasn't going to make a fortune for its author even with the new Public Lending Bill being passed.

Did you know that a gnome was defined by the Elizabethan critic Henry Peacham (1675?–1643?, which leaves him pretty open to question, too) as "pertaining to the manners and common practices of men which declareth, with an apt brevity, what in this life ought to be done, and what not"? This, to me, was a completely new slant on gnomes; "apt brevity" I took to refer to their stunted growth, but I had no idea that all these little toadstool-squatters fancied themselves as models of what the rest of us ought to be doing or not doing. "By their very nature" the tome went on "gnomes belong to the dawn of civilisation; their naïveté and simplicity betrays it."

You could have knocked me down with a feather; I had no idea, except that anyone who keeps on fishing on dry land must be fairly naïve. "It would be an error to suppose" the tome continued "that all gnomes were of a solemn character; some were voluptuous and some chivalrous". Well, now, fancy. I'd never thought of gnomes as solemn; the ones whose paths I cross were still laughing themselves fit to bust even when ASLEF was playing up about flexible rostering and Geoffrey Howe was saying there was a glimmer of light at the end of the tunnel even if we couldn't afford a Channel one. Voluptuous ... well, one of the gnomes in the front garden of "Teesmaid" has a pretty Leslie Phillips glint in his eye but is staring directly at a clump of hepatica; chivalrous ... I suppose so, or they'd have done something about the cats.

I'd only read another couple of hundred pages when I began to get this feeling that I was wasting my time. "This is hopeless," I said to the Head Librarian.

"It says absolutely nothing about why they sit on toadstools, why they keep on grinning when they haven't caught a fish in years, why they're forever pushing wheelbarrows with nothing in them."

"Oh, you mean *those* sort of gnomes?" said the Head Librarian. "I thought, being a literary gentleman, you meant the gnomes of the gnomic poets; you know, Xenophon was one of the first, and Professor Gilbert Murray wrote a most interesting essay on them, particularly the ones collated in the 4th century BC by Lobon of Argos. You mean those ghastly little things people put in their gardens? No, we've nothing on them, I'm afraid. Try the Lending Library downstairs. The Children's Section. Enid Blyton might be a help."

I didn't. Instead, I made a tour of the purlieus of Hove, concentrating on inland gardens rather than the ones down on the front or near the main streets where things like gnomes are apt to disappear overnight. I saw:

17 gnomes sitting on toadstools, most of them looking not unlike Roy Jenkins.
11 gnomes fishing with not a drop of water anywhere near them.
 4 gnomes pushing empty wheelbarrows in various directions.
 1 gnome carrying another gnome piggy-back, both of them laughing their heads off.
 1 gnome wearing over his balaclava what appeared to be a sunflower.
 1 gnome, I regret to say, taken short and relieving himself on the lawn in the manner of the well

known Mannekin Pis statuette in Brussels.

1 gnome lying flat on its back having obviously been sent a purler by a kiddiecar or worse, with its head some eight feet away in the rockery, still laughing itself silly.

Now each of these, and millions more like them, brings pleasure to someone. I just cannot understand why. And I'm the one who's missing out. I faithfully attended Miss Knox's Academy for the Sons and Daughters of Gentlefolk in Berwick-upon-Tweed, but Miss Knox must have skipped the basics. Not only do I fail to understand, let alone appreciate, the raison d'être for gnomes; I cannot read shorthand or music, unravel either a knitting pattern or a chess problem— both of which in print look much the same to me—or work out how many doubles and trebles there are in a yankee.

These are serious shortcomings, and it's not seeing the point of gnomes that really gets me down. But bearing in mind there may be many readers who hold them in high esteem, not one word will I have said against them. They are dear, sweet, lovable little creatures, and may God bless their snug little jerkins. I just wish when they're angling they'd move nearer water, and when pushing wheelbarrows wipe that smile off their face.

A cheerful little red-cheeked gnome
  Was stolen one night from the home
(Or garden, rather) of Aunt Bess—
The Laurels, Scargill Road, Skegness.

Aunt Bess, a built-in snob and prig,
Considered all gnomes infra dig;
Not things one readily forgives
On lawns of true Conservatives.

But this gnome was, in fact, a gift
From her near neighbour, Mrs. Swift,
A splendid lady who had been
Presented to HM the Queen.

Aunt Bess accordingly revised
Her views on gnomes she'd criticised.
If Mrs Swift had thought them so
They must be surely *comme il faut*.

Though when the kleptomaniac struck
She scarcely could believe her luck.
"Thank God!" she cried. "This proves, my word,
That gnomes are for the common herd."

Time passed. Aunt B was summoned to
A Buck House garden party do
Where on the lawns where guests may roam
She saw, to her surprise, a gnome . . .

Just like that nicked from her abode,
The gnomes which once graced Scargill Road.
Might Charles have swiped it, under stress...?
Perish the thought, said loyal Bess.

She stooped down, creaking in her bones,
When—proffering a plate of scones—
Ma'am said "Don't curtsey. Please, no fuss.
I see you're fond of gnomes, like us?

"At Windsor, Sandringham, Balmoral
We've gnomes galore 'midst borders floral
And Philip, Charles, and even Anne
Are all gnome-crazy to a man."

The net result you all can guess:
As soon as Bess regained Skegness
Her garden, back and front, was full
Of gnomes on lawns and round the pool.

Gnomes grinning, angling, pushing barrows
Were dotted through the swedes and marrows;
Hundreds of gnomes of every order
Squatted in her herbaceous border.

Verses like these should end with morals:
When Mrs Swift walks past The Laurels
"Dear God!..." she says. "Each time I pass—
Those *gnomes*!... they're too, too lower-class."

Plots

MOST OF US, thank goodness, have our own garden plots, however humble. Plots about gardens are comparatively rare. Enid Bagnold wrote *The Chalk Garden*, which personally I found almost as hard to get through as taking a spade to its title. There was *The Garden of Allah*, but that was more sensual than cultural; someone, I suppose, must have written *Mrs Wiggs of the Cabbage Patch*. After that, you have to think. If only one or two of our leading dramatists had found time to knock off a horticultural hit...

THESE HAPPY BREEDERS
by
Noel Coward

A roof-garden in Belgravia. L, a cocktail cabinet. R, a sophisticated arrangement of celastrus (bittersweet).

He	Daphne, darling, Rose knows.
She	About—[*pause*] *us*?
He	She's naming you as grounds for a transplant.
She	You mean—[*pause*] it'll all be raked over?

Why?

He   Iris was in Bury St Edmunds the night we flattened Norfolk.

She   You mean—[*pause*] when we were mulching?

He   Don't be vulgar, darling. Cross-pollinating. Hyacinth must have been skulking in the shrubbery when I hoe'd off your top-dressing. She probably had the roses bugged to get us framed. You know what she is—a creeper, a climber. She cultivates beds like Fred Loads. If ever anyone needed dead-heading, she does.

She   How do you—[*pause*] *know*?

He   Darling, she's spread it like bonemeal. Not just to Iris, but to Veronica, Jasmine, Viola, Daisy and Poppy. And you know what they're like when they get in a clump together. Rhubarb, rhubarb, rhubarb.

She   Basil, what are we to—[*pause*] *do*?

He   You could go back to William. [*Cynically, stubbing out a nicotiana on a gardenia.*] Sweet William . . .

She   Darling, he's a weed. He's the narcissus type: willowy. Ever since he came into his father's allotment, he's gone completely to seed.

He   He's very rich—one of the aster family. And he's in a plum job.

She   I wouldn't care if he owned the mint. I'd rather have someone with a little honesty and thrift.

He   Who?

She	Yew. If you think I'm going to start propagating with that grafter again—[*breaking off*] who's that, out on the verandah behind the jacaranda?
Rose	[*singing, off*] London Pride has been handed down to us . . . London Pride is a—
She	*Rose!* . . . prick out, for God's sake. Speedwell. [*ROSE enters*] Rose, darling, you're looking blooming.
Rose	Daphne, I think you'd better know. Basil has been a hardy annual for years now in the same bed as Primrose, Mignonette, Violet, Pansy and Lily. What's more, he's a hybrid—a sucker for leatherjackets. It was all in the *News of the World*—and *Amateur Gardening*. I took some cuttings.
She	Basil, if Rose isn't rambling, I shall have you turfed out.
He	In that case, there's only one thing to say. Myosotis.
She	*Myosotis?*
He	Forget-me-not, darling.
	He exits.
She	Well, that's the blight got rid of. Have a drink, Rose, dear.
Rose	Thank you, darling. Just a small juniper and citrus.

CURTAIN

Or on slightly heavier soil . . .

THE PRUNUS ORCHARD
by
Anton Chekhov

A crazy paving near Omsk. L, a samovar. R, a collective arrangement of Siberian wallflowers.

Tanya	The cherry blossom is out, Vanya.
Vanya	Thank you, little Tanya. But my shoes are all right.
Tanya	I mean the prunus in the orchard. And *Tass* says it's eighteen degrees below zero. I don't understand it.
Vanya	It's these satellites they keep sending up, little Tanya. The only things anyone dares send up in this country. Before the satellites, the weather toe'd the Party line ... export freeze in the winter, then a thaw, detente in the summer, cold war again in the winter. Now you might be living in Edgbaston ...
Tanya	And Mme Ranovsky coming home ... today, with the prunus out! ...
Vanya	Never mind the prunus. Is the vodka out?
Tanya	Natch.
Vanya	She loved her prunus, did Mme Ranovsky. She used to place the stones round the edge of her plate of borsch and count ... this year's Five Year Plan, the next Five Year Plan, some goddam other Five Year Plan, surely, and then *niet*.

	When it came to "niet" eight times running, she ran off.
Tanya	You can't say prunus didn't make her go.
Vanya	Now the orchard's to be turned into a caravan camping site, run by Intourist, special cheap return fares here and back by Aeroflot. She won't like it. Topless peasants and transistors blaring out the Rolling Steppes until four in the morning. The Tsar wouldn't have liked it.
Tanya	Anna Karenina wouldn't have liked it.
Vanya	Andropov would hate it.

Sleigh-bells and the crack of whips on serfs' backs, OFF.

Tanya	She's here! . . .
Vanya	Compose yourself, child. Think of Tchaikovsky. And don't ask how little Eyolf is. He was Ibsen.

MME RANOVSKY *enters.*

Mme R	Home, at last! . . . the train was four hours late. Flexible roster trouble at Kiev. Home, to my orchard . . . with the snow falling and the prunus in bloom, just as it was the night I left for Paris, met that rich Georgian commissar with the salt-mine franchise, lived with him in the villa at Menton until I found he was a friend of Philby's, returned to Moscow and was Diaghilev's inspiration for *Les Biches*.
Tanya	I told you prunus made her go.
Mme R	How is Danya?
Vanya	He defected. To the KGB.
Mme R	And Stanya?

Tanya	He asked for political asylum. They put him in a loony-bin.
Mme R	Time stands still. Only the rouble changes. You know you can get deep-freeze take-away prunus flan now in GUM? [BUTLINSKY, *a rich landowner, enters*] Butlinsky! . . . what are you doing here?
But	Camping.
Mme R.	I had enough of that with the Bolshoi, thank you.
But	I mean the orchard. The prunus orchard. We could get four hundred mobile homes out there, each accommodating six intourists, eight in high season, at sixty roubles a week, plus entrance fees for communal swimming-pool, crazy golf, Russian roulette, and a campsite shop selling bogus caviar and phoney folk murals from the Urals. You'n'me splitting fifty-fifty, Little Mother of All the Russians. Whadya say?
Mme R	You'll find the agreement already signed, over there in the politburo. And less of the Little Mother of All the Russians, comrade. There were others at it.

CURTAIN

Or, of course, the Bard . . .

THIS BLESSED PLOT
by
William Shakespeare

A garden in Arden. L, Anne Hathaway's cottage. R, rosemary for remembrance. 1st and 2nd GARDENERS trying to work out the plot.

1st G	Ho, there! . . .
2nd G	Since earliest blush of fair Aurora's rays
	Cast dappled light o'er dew-encrusted fields
	And, like a wakened mother giving suck,
	Warmed with her kiss all Nature's progeny
	Spreading dawn's blessed light on meadows green,
	On hills and hedgerows, valleys, copses, dales,
	Rousing from long night's sleep each growing thing
	From mighty oak to tend'rest columbine,
	From ancient elm to seedlings newly-sown
	And in this very garden made the soil
	Which but an hour ago was cold and chill
	Alive again and vibrant, warmed anew,
	Each single thing within it bursting forth
	To bring new pleasure to another day . . .
	Since, as I said before, dawn's early light
	I have been hoeing, dammit.
1st G	But soft! . . . who comes?
	Perdita, by my troth!

139

2nd G	Perdition take her! For she thinks she knows
	Each flower, each bush, the name of every shrub,
	And what is more the care that each one needs,
	That to be tended thus, this to be pruned just so,
	The roses fed and water'd in her way
	And no-one else's. Of all a garden's pests
	There's none more pestilential than the wench
	Who knows it all. Small wonder, years ago,
	"The Winter's Tale" was damned for its langueurs
	When fair Perdita in Act IV, Scene 4,
	Babbled at length on plants and flowers and seeds
	Hoping to 'stablish 'gainst all doubts she knew
	More than her hard-worked gardeners ever do.
	PERDITA *enters.*
Perdita	Good morrow, gardeners. Ah, those marigolds
	That go to bed wi' the sun and weeping rise
	When he too rises ... they are crowded there,
	Jostling each other as spectators do
	At cockfights. They should be set apart
	So that each single bloom may show itself

	Unelbow'd by its neighbour. See to it, sirrah.
1st G	Yes, ma'am.
Perdita	Those daffodils that come e're swallows do
	And brave March winds with beauty; they look pale and wan
	And but a shadow of their size last year.
	New bulbs I ordered from that firm in Lincs.
	Those are not they, or if those bulbs they be,
	I shall demand my money back. Next Spring, take care.
	I wish the bulbs I ordered planted there
	Not in your own back gardens, changed no doubt
	For near-wild age-old daffs that you've thrown out.
2nd G	Very good, ma'am. I'll see to it, ma'am.
Perdita	Those primroses ... they languish i' the sun.
	They seek the shade and shade we amply have.
	Each hedge o'ergrown, the winter jasmine there
	In need of trimming like a potman's hair.
	The honeysuckle rampant, and the grass
	So high no mole from hill to hill may pass.
	Gardeners at times, though surely highly paid,
	Seem shy of work. Or, if not shy, afraid.

1st G	Sorry, ma'am. Been a lot o' rain this past fortnight, ma'am.
Perdita	These lilies . . . nay, good Adam, not the spade . . .
	Dividing lilies, rules must be obeyed.
	First, gently fork them out; and then each crown
	Must be dissected—Adam, *put it down*! . . .

1st Gardener fells her with his spade. She falls dead on the compost heap.

2nd G	Best morning's work we ever put in, mate. Right: start diggin'.

CURTAIN

Tidying Up

THE MOVING FINGER writes and, having writ, there comes the un-nerving moment when proofs must be checked and the writer has to re-read, if not actually eat, his words. Re-reading these ones, I seem to come out of them not just as a hopelessly amateur gardener but also as an extremely disgruntled, crotchety and cantankerous one. Complaints, complaints, complaints. I have more green-fly than anyone else; when I spray the roses for black spot the leaves turn yellow and fall off while the spots move on to another rose; my neighbours on both sides, who after all are only trying to be helpful, are dismissed as pests; no-one who borrows anything returns it; advertisers outdo the Tichbourne character in making false claims, and the entire chemical industry is suspect; house plants lose all self-control but still control the house and the people living in it; even the lady of the house is criticised for wasting time chatting them up. The man obviously gets precious little pleasure out of his garden, and doesn't deserve to own one.

Now that we're at the checking-out stage, let me at least correct *that*, while no doubt leaving a few mis-spellings uncorrected and the odd semi-colon where it should never have been in the first place. Hand on heart, I can honestly say that the gardens I have looked after or neglected—and many better-kept ones belonging to other people—have brought me more genuine, lasting delight than a rapturous first-night reception (and that was a long time ago) or even the occasional fan who still sidles up and says can she have your autograph, please, it's not for herself, it's for her little niece who's eight and in hospital so she's not particular whose she gets, but we never missed one of those lovely *A to Z* shows you did on telly before you got past it, so in our family your name's still a household word, Mr Melford.

Without wishing to tread on the path so well trodden by Mr Nichols, there is no greater pleasure, no more satisfying sense of achievement, than to meander round your own garden, however humble, on say a warm June evening, sniff the rival perfumes, be amazed for the thousandth time at the absolute perfection of a "Peace" rose midway between the bud and the blowsy stage, and saying "Well, it is looking rather nice—and it's *mine*." Adding *sotto voce* in case the neighbours are listening, either "and alone I did it", "I did it my way", or some other sweeping statement denying any co-operation on the part of Nature, the weather, the much-maligned chemical industry,or the commendable private enterprise shown by plants themselves.

The great thing—or one of the many great things— about a garden is that neither size nor space nor the spending of money makes in the long run all that difference. You may own a vast estate with rolling lawns and a herbaceous border the length of

Southend pier; you may, as I do, have a town garden not much bigger than a Guinness poster on the hoardings (plus, of course, in my case, a back passage); individually, the end products are exactly the same. Daffodils look every bit as good in a small front patch as in the spacious grounds of a stately home; winter jasmine comes out dead on cue in the do-it-yourself back garden as it does in the ones with three under-gardeners and the odd-job man who trims the hedges when he's not driving the boss to the station to catch the 9.47 and picking him up again when he gets home exhausted on the 3.40.

In fact, being simple myself, it seems to me that very often the simplest things to grow give the most pleasure. A couple of yards from my desk at this very moment there is a vase containing the last of this season's gladioli and an arrangement of plain, ordinary, common-or-garden nicotiana and cornflowers. The gladioli originally cost quite a lot of money; each year they've been cosseted, kept dry and warm in seed-boxes under the staging in the greenhouse, with the boxes lovingly lined with old copies of the *Observer*; the tobacco plant and the cornflowers naturally came from packets of seed scattered nonchalantly in trays of compost, pricked out when their time came and shoved in where they were expected to perform. Even the Fletchley Horticultural Society's judges would be hard put to it to decide which of the three was the most decorative. (My money, in fact, would go on the tobacco plant; it's a greatly underestimated flower for cutting, even if the stems are a bit gummy.)

Out on the table in that by now notorious back

passage there has been this year what was planned as a tasteful arrangement of pendulum begonias and that silvery-leaved miniature cineraria. At the last moment there were thumbed in three, I think, nursturtium seeds heard rattling at the foot of an old seed packet. What was by far the most successful member of the ensemble? Which lasted longest and gave the most pleasure? The poor relation; the often despised nasturtium. Such a graceful display, visitors said after being primed with a couple of gins and then forced to do the conducted tour; the way those tendrils drape themselves over the edge of the table, it's so artistic, you should team up with Moyses Stevens and Constance Spry, no, honestly, we're not kidding.

It's another sign, I suppose, of a simple nature, but year after year—and Heaven knows we've been getting at the weeds now for around sixty of them (I didn't start weeding until comparatively late in life)— I never cease to be amazed by the miracle of it all. Have you ever examined—critically, I mean—the average begonia tuber, not necessarily one of those unhappily named after myself? It's not what you'd call attractive. There is not the slightest hint of the pleasure in store and the beauty ahead. Let's face it, it's usually roughly the shape of the Isle of Man and looks like Malcolm Muggeridge. Yet out of that knobbly, apparently dead-as-a-dodo-or-doornail misshapen little lump there comes, in order, the pale pink shoot, then the ridiculously slender stem which has to do its best to jack up a load far too heavy for it, and finally (especially if you get rid of the males) the most gorgeous blooms the circumference of a soup plate. Well, a side plate. All right, then, a saucer. It's a miracle, and we take it for granted.

Gardeners take a great deal for granted. We put in a few dozen new muscari or snowdrops and assume that by January next year they'll start coming up; few of us lose sleep thinking that, if Nature went about her business in the same way as ASLEF or NUPE or SOGAT, they might just as well start going down. In, say, late September. A handful of wizened, shrivelled-up little objects results in bunch after bunch of the most glorious sweet peas with a much more exclusive perfume than those the lady of the house spends a fortune on; we say isn't it dreadful, the way the price of seeds keeps going up every year!

A garden is not only a lovesome thing; when you think about it, it's awesome. For one thing, here is this crotchety, curmudgeonly old gentleman being positively mellow, even grateful. It's a miracle all right.

It also occurred to me, correcting the grammatical errors but leaving the many horticultural ones untouched, that this is not a book likely to add anything of real practical value to the millions of words already written about gardens and gardening. To the writers of those millions of words it will seem an unforgivably flippant and frivolous way of dealing with what after all is a very serious subject. Most expert gardeners—certainly most expert gardening writers, which is not always the same thing—are tremendously serious about the whole thing. They're public-spirited enough to pass on their expertise, but we can't have any levity about lawns or green-fly gags.

They also—the professional writers, I mean—
ssume that the rest of us have the same facilities and
ime that they have. For many of us, gardening means
ipping out at the end of a hard day's work and
oping to get in the first row of early runners before it
ets too dark. And then planning to have a good,
olid weekend at it, but somehow never getting
ound to it what with promising to give old Arthur a
ame of golf and Sandown races being on the telly on
he Saturday afternoon.

The experts—the *real* gardeners—get, I'm sure,
mmense satisfaction out of their gardens; I doubt if
hey get much fun. And this is what matters. The
noment a garden ceases to be enjoyable, becomes a
ore or a chore rather than a delight, that is the time
ither to lay down those concrete slabs or get under
hem. Until that unhappy moment—however badly
he species known so strangely as *homo sapiens*
ehaves—it is as near a certainty as you are likely to
et that the miracle will happen again and go on
appening. Next Spring the honeysuckle will once
nore be in danger of being charged with riotous and
isorderly behaviour all over that Sussex flint wall;
reen-fly or no green-fly (what an absurd thing to say:
o green-fly?) the lilies and the roses will look as
ood as ever and smell as good as ever; the first
npertinent little shoots will pop up on the fuchsia
ou thought had been finally killed off by the frost.
nd kind, thoughtful, helpful neighbours will say
ou do know, don't you, that the trouble with those
Michelmas daisies is powdery mildew and what you
vant to do if they're not too far gone, which by the
ooks of them they are, is spray 'em with a solution of

benomyl and dinocap.

You can't keep a really good miracle down
Whatever sort of garden you have, small or large
chalk or clay, level or terraced, enjoy it and have fun
That, after all, is what they're there for.

A garden is a lovesome thing,
God wot...
Rose plot, black spot,
Bulb rot,
The *lot*.

Blight on the beeches,
Earwigs in dahlias,
Leaf curl on peaches,
Gall in azaleas.

Canker in apple trees,
Eelworm in spuds,
First sign of rust disease
On hollyhock buds.

Blotch on the hellebore,
Slugworms in gherkins,
Greenfly and thrips galore
On Dorothy Perkins.

Wilt on the brassicas,
Mildew on pears,
Moles staging massacres
On lawns—but who cares?

Groundsel is flourishing,
Chickweed's no slouch.
No need for nourishing
Plantain or couch.

Thistles are doing well.
Liverwort thrives.
Bindweed is utter hell.
We've ants in the chives.

A garden is a Paradise
And God created Eden,
You must believe, for more than Eve
To breed in.